THE
NO-GUILT
GUIDE
TO
WITNESSING

D0064340

THE
NO-GUILT
GUIDE
TO
WITNESSING

GEORGE SWEETING

While intended for the reader's personal
enjoyment and instruction, this book is
also for group study. A leader's guide
with Reproducible Response Sheets is
available from your local bookstore or
from the publisher.

VICTOR BOOKS ®
A DIVISION OF SCRIPTURE PRESS PUBLICATIONS INC.
USA CANADA ENGLAND

Library of Congress Cataloging-in-Publication Data

Sweeting, George, 1924-
    The no-guilt guide to witnessing / by George Sweeeting.
      p.   cm.
    ISBN 0-89693-400-4
    1. Witness bearing (Christianity) I. Title.
BV4520.S94   1991
248'.5—dc20   90-22299
                                         CIP

CONTENTS

24372

PREFACE

Too often an unnecessary burden of guilt is placed on Christians in regard to witnessing. Though probably unintentional, the idea is conveyed that Christians are somehow responsible for results. However, the Bible clearly implies that God alone is "the Lord of the harvest" (Matt. 9:38) and that God "makes things grow" (1 Cor. 3:7).

This perspective is seen throughout this book and enlarged in chapter 12, "Are We Responsible for Results?" The parable presents the sower, the seed, and the soil. The sower appears to be anyone who sows the good Gospel seed. The seed is simply the Gospel. The all-important element is the soil which determines the results.

Perhaps by nature you are shy. Or you are a new Christian with little or no experience in witnessing. The challenge from Jesus is to sow the good seed anyway. The point is not your talent, intelligence, or charisma, but rather the divine power of the seed and the Spirit-prepared soil that results in a harvest. Results are God's prerogative while faithfulness is your responsibility. "The fruit of the righteous is a tree of life, and he who wins souls is wise" (Prov. 11:30).

Now some suggestions for using this book:

1. *Read it alone.* This book is designed to help you in your personal preparation for sharing your faith with others. To enjoy success in witnessing, you must have a desire and commitment to the task. I urge you not to rush through this material. Study it carefully day by day and allow the Spirit of God to guide you as you apply what you read.

2. *Study it with a friend.* Our Lord's pattern for evangelism was to send out the seventy, two by two, "into every city and place" (Luke 10:1). It can be rewarding to study and interact

with a friend as you seek to apply these principles in team witnessing.

3. *Use it in a group study.* The fourteen lessons found in this book are designed for use in an adult Sunday School class or for home Bible studies.

Christians fail to witness primarily for two reasons: fear and lack of know-how. This book will help you overcome both of these obstacles. It is my earnest prayer that because of this study, you will be encouraged and equipped to share the good news faithfully.

ACKNOWLEDGEMENTS

I want to express my warm appreciation to Dr. Leonard Rascher and Dr. Dennis Fisher, both faculty members of the Moody Bible Institute, for reading and commenting on the original manuscript. And thanks to my son and pastor, the Rev. Donald Sweeting, for critiquing the manuscript, and to my faithful secretary, Beth Jesel, for typing and proofreading it.

I have never found witnessing to come naturally and easily. Some of you may find this difficult to believe, but by nature I'm a shy, reserved person; initiating conversations with strangers is sometimes difficult for me. . . .

I don't even know if evangelism is my spiritual gift.

What I do know is that God has made it crystal clear in His Word that every Christian is to "go and make disciples in all nations. . . ."

> Bill Bright *(Witnessing without Fear,* Here's Life Publishers, p. 18)

I determined that as I loved Christ, and as Christ loved souls, I would press Christ on the individual soul, so that none who were in the proper sphere of my individual responsibility or influence should lack the opportunity of meeting the question whether or not they would individually trust and follow Christ. The resolve I made was, that whenever I was in such intimacy with a soul as to be justified in choosing my subject of conversation, the theme of themes should have prominence between us, so that I might learn his need, and if possible, meet it.

That decision has largely shaped my Christian lifework.

> Henry Clay Trumbull (quoted in *Taking Men Alive,* G.G. Trumbull, Fleming H. Revell, p. 68)

ONE
How I Began to Witness

G etting started is a challenge, whether it's learning to ride a bicycle, getting into the water for a swim, or daily physical exercise. Each requires a conscious decision and effort to begin.

Probably the number one obstacle to sharing our Christian faith is *fear*. Fear of failure, fear of being rejected, and even the fear of offending the person we want to help. It's safer to remain silent and withhold our witness. Each of us struggles with fear. I have help for you.

Another reason for failing to witness is the lack of know-how. Adequate preparation is the answer to this obstacle. Preparation provides poise in sharing the Good News. This book will help you prepare.

A third obstacle to witnessing is a misunderstanding of what God requires of us. Though we all enjoy seeing the results, we are called to faithfully sow the good seed regardless of the response. When I understood this, I was liberated to witness naturally and attractively.

I came alive to the Christian life as a teenager. A verse of

Scripture grabbed me with such force that I couldn't escape its message. The verse was, "Do not merely listen to the word, and so deceive yourselves. Do what it says" (James 1:22). Although I was familiar with the teachings of the Bible, I neglected to obey the truth I claimed to believe. On that particular day I promised the Lord that I would "do what it says."

A PERSONAL RELATIONSHIP NEEDED

The starting point in the adventure of sharing the Good News is the new birth. Without a spiritual birth, we are dead, and dead things can't grow. Witnessing is primarily sharing the new life we have in Christ; it is impossible to share what we don't have. Unless we know Jesus Christ in a personal way and enjoy His life within, we will find it impossible to share with others about Him.

It is possible to say the right things about Jesus, and even share what constitutes the Gospel or quote Bible verses, but sharing about Jesus and sharing Jesus are two different things. Uncertainty or insincerity will result in failure. Each witness must possess the inner assurance of a personal relationship with Christ.

A COMMITMENT TO WITNESS

As a child, I made a profession of faith in Christ. To the best of my understanding, I committed my life to Him. But like many others, I was self-centered, and often insensitive to the teaching of Scripture. Ego still ruled my life. I had my own plans and was committed to accomplishing them.

During the month of August some decades ago in a special church series, I made a commitment to "seek first the kingdom of God." I clearly recall that I had a strong desire to be alone where I could listen to God and seek whatever guidance He might have for my life. That night I spent time with my pastor, talking about God's will for my life.

To get to my boyhood home meant a bus ride of ten miles and an additional three-mile walk. The ride and walk were different that night as I felt carried along by the excitement of my new calling. That bus ride and walk gave me my special time alone with God.

My mother was the kind of parent who never went to bed until all her six children were home and settled. That night she seemed intuitively to realize that something life-changing had taken place in my life. She shared warmly about spiritual matters, and then we knelt by her special chair to pray, as she asked for God's unique guidance in my life.

My bedroom was a small ten feet by ten feet unheated room that had once been part of the attic. That night alone in my room as I knelt to pray, I wrote down my first goals, four of them. Although I considered myself an average teenager, these goals that came to mind have intensified over the years. They are:

1. *Seek* to bring glory to God. (1 Cor. 10:31).
2. *Cultivate* the inner life (2 Peter 3:18).
3. *Disciple* as many people as humanly possible (Matt. 28:19-20).
4. *Win* as many people to faith in Jesus Christ as possible (Prov. 11:30).

Today, many years later, these still constitute my *lifetime goal.*

As I knelt, aglow with divine love, I promised to become a faithful follower and witness. My commitment was as serious and as total as I knew how.

The very next day, I began to share the Good News at my high school in Paterson, New Jersey. Most of my schoolmates, like Paul who sat next to me in mechanical drawing class, were not Christians. He was a likable friend, and I was concerned about his spiritual future, but where would I start and how would I begin a meaningful conversation? What would Paul think of me? What would I say if he just happened to show interest? Those were just a few of the questions racing through my mind.

WISE COUNSEL

I was privileged to grow up in a church where we enjoyed a caring teaching ministry. Our pastor's sermons were life-building, and relevant to our needs. He was a choice role model for the youth of the church. He and his spiritually minded lay people were continually sharing Christ in the community and encouraging the young people to do the same. We were well-grounded concerning the person and work of Christ so that our witnessing was the natural overflow of a living relationship with Christ.

The youth and sponsors of our church formed a group to conduct services in missions, small churches, hospitals, and wherever people would welcome us. That not only encouraged our commitment, but provided a workshop to learn by doing.

Each of us were encouraged to write out in simple language our conversion experience. We then condensed our testimony to a three-minute presentation and we committed it to memory. This enabled us to share with confidence a well thought-out verbal witness.

Attractive literature was recommended to assist us in a conversation. The first booklet I used was "Safety, Certainty and Enjoyment" by George Cutting. Equipped with a few copies, I went off to school seeking divine guidance. I'll never forget my very first try. "Paul," I said, "here's a booklet that means a lot to me. Please read it and tell me tomorrow what you think of it." Paul, without hesitation, took the booklet and promised to read it. In fact, he was flattered that I was interested in his life. It was a weak start, but it was a start. The booklet I gave him begins:

You are traveling—traveling from time into eternity. And who knows how near you may be this moment to the final terminal? Let me ask you then, "What class are you traveling?" There are just three.

First class—those who are saved and know it.

Second class—those who are not sure of salvation but anxious to be so.

Third class—those who are not only unsaved but totally indifferent about it.

The next day, Paul told me that he was in the second class, not sure of salvation but anxious to have assurance. Because I was shy and fearful of what others might think or say, I invited Paul to my home after school, where at least I could attempt to answer his questions in the quietness and privacy of my room. Fear is normal and universal. We're all fearful. I was fearful for at least three reasons. First, I was afraid of being personally rejected and maybe mocked. Secondly, I was afraid that Jesus might be rejected because of my limitations. And third, I feared that Paul might be unimpressed, and consider neither of us worth accepting or rejecting.

MAKING THE APPLICATION

Because I was a beginner, I witnessed with simple, plain, understandable words. Words like "redemption" and "propitiation" are great words that we prize, but not for communicating our faith to others. Sick souls need simple words. Beware of scaring people off by pompous words and tired out cliches.

Witnessing, of course, includes infinitely more than rattling off verses of Scripture. It includes first of all *what I am*, as well as what I do and what I say. Some Christians tend to be "all life" and "no lip" while others are "all lip" and "no life." A powerful combination is "living" and "lipping" the Good News. Witnessing involves sharing in a natural, understandable way "who Jesus is" and "what He has done." It is telling people that Jesus is the sinless Son of God who died for the sins of the world, that He arose from the grave and wants to be involved in our daily lives.

In a simple way, I told Paul all I knew about Jesus. To the best of my ability I presented the way of salvation, supporting it with familiar passages of Scripture.

First, I showed Paul the *spiritual condition of the entire human race.* I read Romans 3:23, "For all have sinned, and fall short of the glory of God." I then turned to Isaiah 53:6 and read, "We all, like sheep, have gone astray, each of us has turned to his own way; and the Lord has laid on Him the iniquity of us all."

Second, I explained who Jesus is and what He accomplished for all mankind. Together we read John 14:6, "Jesus answered, I am the way and the truth and the life. No one comes to the Father except through Me." That was followed by reading John 3:16, "For God so loved the world that He gave His one and only Son, that whoever believes in Him shall not perish but have eternal life."

Then I talked about what it means to believe. We looked at the words of Peter, "Repent, then, and turn to God, so that your sins may be wiped out" (Acts 3:19).

The reading of Scripture and the Holy Spirit did their work, for Paul was ready to commit himself to Jesus Christ. Simply and beautifully, he welcomed Jesus into his life and became by faith a child of God. I will never forget that happy day.

Over the years I have seen Paul as he has grown spiritually strong. In spite of my fears and inexperience, God used that faithful witness. Paul was the first of more than a dozen class-mates I had the thrill of introducing to faith in Jesus Christ.

OBEYING JESUS

The first instructions Jesus gave to His followers were, "Come ... after Me, and I will make you to become fishers of men" (Mark 1:17). His last instruction while on earth to His disciples was, "But you will receive power when the Holy Spirit comes on you; and you will be my witnesses in Jerusalem, and in all Judea and Samaria, and to the ends of the earth" (Acts 1:8). Jesus *began* and *ended* His earthly ministry with the command that His followers should be *witnesses.* A witness is one who gives testimony on behalf of another. It is the privilege and right of Christians to affirm the reality of Christ in their daily life.

Will Houghton, the fourth president of the Moody Bible Institute, often said, "Our only excuse for living is to be a witness." Our number one purpose in life is to bring glory to God, and Spirit-guided witnessing accomplishes that purpose. When Moses went to Pharoah he asked, "Let my people go, that they may serve me" (Ex. 9:1). God freed His ancient people, in order that they would *serve* Him. The old motto is true, "We are saved to serve." Remember this: each believer in Jesus Christ is commanded to share the Gospel with his world. While recognizing that fact, we must remember that our abilities differ. And yet we must not let that become an excuse for not witnessing but rather accept the challenge to improve our God-given gifts, some of which may be still unknown.

It is also important that each of us sincerely give ourselves to people so that we can sense and feel their needs. Each individual is different and must be approached with an understanding of their individuality.

Here are some suggestions:

● Prepare a list of friends who need to know Jesus Christ.

● Pray for them each day by name.

● Attempt to become involved with them in some type of everyday activity.

● Seek to reflect the Christian faith in ordinary human kindness.

● Share some choice, attractive Christian literature with your friends.

● Tactfully tell them what Jesus means to you and how they too can discover His presence in their lives.

Remember also that God in His goodness is ready and able to

use each of us just as we are. With God's strength, *you can be* a faithful witness.

I have discovered that it is next to impossible to steer a parked car, so may I warmly encourage you to *begin* witnessing faithfully! Start where you are, with what you know, but do *start*. The best way to begin is to *begin*, and the best time to begin is . . . NOW!

REMINDERS

● Witnessing involves sharing "who Jesus is" and "what He has done."

● No one can witness concerning Jesus Christ successfully until he or she has been converted.

● Each believer in Jesus Christ is commissioned to share the Gospel with his world.

● The successful combination is "living" and "lipping" the Good News.

● It is hard to steer a parked car, so I urge you to get moving!

Yes, love is the magic key of life — not to get what we want, but to become what we ought to be.

> Eileen Guder (*To Live in Love*, Zondervan, p. 18)

I took up that word *Love*, and I do not know how many weeks I spent in studying the passages in which it occurs, till at last I could not help loving people. It just flowed out my fingertips.

> D. L. Moody (quoted in *Bush Aglow*, R.E. Day, Judson Press, p. 146)

Love this world through me, Lord,
This world of broken men;
Thou didst love through death, Lord,
Oh, love in me again!
Souls are in despair, Lord,
Oh, make me know and care;
When my life they see,
May they behold Thee;
Oh, love the world through me.

> Will Houghton (quoted in *A Watchman on the Wall*, Wilbur M. Smith, Eerdmans, p. 186)

Do you know the world is dying
For a little bit of love?
Everywhere we hear them sighing,
For a little bit of love.

> Anonymous

TWO

Make Love Your Aim

During my student days at Chicago's Moody Bible Institute, I was seriously ill. Our school doctor, Titus Johnson, recommended immediate surgery for the removal of a grapefruit-sized tumor. Because it was believed to be malignant, the operation was followed by thirty radiation treatments. I shall always remember the warm, loving concern of Doctor Johnson. Carefully he explained that my sickness could be fatal, and if not, the possibilities of my fathering children were remote.

My bed at Chicago's Swedish Covenant Hospital was, in a real sense, my altar of sacrifice. I reminded the Lord of my commitment to serve Him. I told Him that I wanted His will for my life more than anything in this world. I prayed, "Dear Lord, this bed is my altar. Adjust my life to Your supreme purpose. If it's according to Your will, allow me to be a *living* sacrifice. I dedicate myself to be a channel of Your love."

During those hospital days, one of my former Sunday School teachers, John Roe, sent me a booklet by James McConkey on the power of God's love. As I read it, I began to see my great lack in this area. The combination of sickness, pain, loneliness, the sights and sounds of the hospital, and the booklet about God's love were all blended by the Great Physician to open me up to the power of God's love. Through it all, I caught a vision of the exciting possibility of becoming an instrument of God's love to my generation.

In the years since those crisis days, I have enjoyed for the most part, good health, a strong body, and the unexpected gifts of four sons. Dr. Titus Johnson wrote me, reminding that God had provided in a miraculous way.

Most of us realize the importance of sharing our faith in a caring way, but the big question is how? How can I convey to others a sense of caring? How can I become an instrument of God's love?

Each of us realizes that the source of all love is God Himself. "God is love," and we must begin this quest by receiving Jesus Christ as Lord and Savior, and cultivating a knowledge of God.

FIVE STEPS RELATING TO LOVE

Here are five practical steps that "follow after love" (1 Cor. 14:1).

1. *Make God's love your aim.* Repeatedly the Bible affirms the supremacy of God's love guiding and motivating our lives in all we do. Love is the number one reason for all service in Christ's name (2 Cor. 5:14).

Paul called this divine love "a more excellent way" (1 Cor. 12:31). Of all the gifts listed in 1 Corinthians 12, "love" is the greatest. Faith may have priority, but love has preeminence. Paul reminds us that love supersedes faith (1 Cor. 13:13), that faith will climax in sight, whereas "love never fails" (1 Cor. 13:8).

Love is also greater than eloquence, the gift of prophecy, knowledge, faith, acts of benevolence, and even martyrdom (1 Cor. 13:1-3). God's love is without question the greatest.

John called this love "a new commandment" (John 13:34)

and said it was to be *the mark* that would distinguish Jesus' disciples. "By this all men will know that you are My disciples, if you love one another" (John 13:35).

The Apostle Peter also underscored and announced the priority of love. "Above all, love each other deeply, because love covers over a multitude of sins" (1 Peter 4:8). Above all that Peter had taught is God's love ruling and reigning in our lives. Nothing supersedes this.

If love becomes our aim, then consciously and subconsciously you will "follow the way of love" (1 Cor. 14:1). The word *follow* is a strenuous word. It calls for an all-out effort. When we understand the place and importance of this love, it is easier to remember that we must witness in this spirit. So make love your aim. It is the peak of all gifts. May nothing hinder your pursuit.

2. *Pray for love.* Each day in my daily devotions I simply ask the Lord for a loving heart. The Apostle Paul encourages us to do this: "And this I pray, that your love may abound yet more and more in knowledge and in all judgment" (Phil. 1:9, KJV). Divine love is not soft or sentimental, but aware, alert, and involved. Paul prayed specifically for an overflowing, abounding love, because without this love we are nothing, and everything we do profits nothing (1 Cor. 13:1-3). We might ask, "Is there anything less than nothing?" Since God's love is the greatest of all God's gifts, we need to pray for abounding love.

3. *Love is a fruit.* Divine love is a fruit of the Holy Spirit. Before natural fruit is developed, it is exposed to sunshine, rain, darkness, wind, and plenty of time. Then after all of this exposure, the ripened fruit appears. Paul reminds us that "the fruit of the Spirit is *love*" (Gal. 5:22). It also takes the trials and tears of life to produce love as a fruit of the Spirit. Though the fruits of the Holy Spirit are several, the first fruit is love.

4. *Allow the Holy Spirit to love through you.* Love is not something we work up or even pray down, but rather it is the natural and spontaneous result of allowing the Holy Spirit of God to

express His love in us. Our natural heart does not love others. The human heart is interested in self and the material things of this world. The secret of loving is discovered in allowing the Holy Spirit to freely love through us.

The Apostle Paul states, "The love of God is shed abroad in our hearts by the Holy Spirit who is given to us" (Rom. 5:5, KJV). The essence of sharing our faith lovingly is found in a submission to God the indwelling Holy Spirit.

5. *Love by faith.* Satan is opposed to faith in Jesus Christ. He did everything in his power to stop you from coming to Him in the first place. And now, after you have received Christ by faith, Satan focuses all his efforts to stop you from continuing a life of faith. What he failed to accomplish before conversion, he often accomplishes after conversion.

At times in life I have had to learn to love others by faith until God stepped in to replace my weak, imperfect feelings with His love. Each believer can ask the Lord to give him the ability to love by faith. Frankly, some people are hard to love. Fredrick the Great is reported to have said, "The better I come to know people, the more I love my dog." C.W. Vanderbergh wrote:

> To love the whole world
> For me's no chore
> My only real problem's
> My neighbor next door.

Recently a young woman came to me for advice. As we talked, she poured out a story of great bitterness toward her parents. After sharing with her from the Scriptures, I was able to lead her to acknowledge Jesus as her personal Savior and Lord. Almost immediately she said, "I want to be reconciled to my parents, but how, how can I ever love them again?"

"By faith," I answered. "Ask the Lord to give you a new love — His love, for your parents." He alone can do this and the good news is over a period of time He did.

Job of the Old Testament was harshly criticized and falsely judged by his so-called friends. At first they sat with him in apparent sympathy and silence. However after seven days they brutally accused him. Ultimately, Job was released from his affliction *when he by faith prayed* for these accusing friends. "After Job had prayed for his friends, the Lord made him prosperous again" (Job 42:10). There are those occasions in life where we can only love by faith and that love begins by earnest prayer for the offenders.

Real love also serves. Love is not content to sit and do nothing. Love is active. It has to express itself in giving, serving, and witnessing. The proof of our love comes in our willingness to share. A high school girl who specialized in cutting down her classmates now sees the selfishness of her ways. She prayed for a God-given desire to understand her friends' shortcomings—as well as her own. She now sincerely prays for them and also shares God's love.

It is also important to remember that we must make time to worship before we work; meditation must precede ministering; being tuned in to the Holy Spirit precedes being tuned in to people. There must always be that quiet space in which our souls are refreshed and prepared for sharing our witness.

The early Christians gave themselves to prayer and communion, which resulted in a spontaneous expansion. How much more do we in this jet age need to sincerely worship Christ before we witness for Christ? "They that wait upon the Lord shall renew their strength; they shall mount up with wings as eagles; they shall run, and not be weary; and they shall walk, and not faint" (Isa. 40:31, kjv). When you are yielded to the Holy Spirit, your worship and witness are blended together. Witnessing is the fruit of worshiping. The fullness of love is the natural overflow of the fullness of the Holy Spirit. Witnessing begins and continues with love. So, make love your aim.

REMINDERS
- Faith has priority, but love has preeminence.
- Love is not something we work up; rather it is allowing the Holy Spirit the chance to love through us.
- The fullness of love is the result of the fullness of the Holy Spirit.
- At times, we must love someone by faith, and then God will step in to transform our weak, imperfect attempt to love.

Isaiah 66:8 tells us that "as soon as Zion travailed she brought forth her children"; and this is the most fundamental element in the work of God. Can children be born without pain? Can there be birth without travail? Yet how many expect in the spiritual realm that which is not possible in the natural!

> Oswald J. Smith (quoted in *The Passion for Souls*, Marshall, Morgan & Scott, p. 26)

I think my soul was never so drawn out in intercession for others as it has been this night; I hardly ever so longed to live to God, and to be altogether devoted to Him; I wanted to wear out my life for Him.

I wrestled for the ingathering of souls, for multitudes of poor souls, personally, in many distant places.

> David Brainerd (quoted in *The Passion for Souls*, p. 32)

THREE
A Passion for Souls

ear gripped the hearts of the people of Amsterdam on May 10, 1940 as the armies of Hitler invaded the Netherlands, Belgium, and Luxembourg. Europe was engulfed in World War II. Three days later, on May 13, Winston Churchill electrified the British parliament and the world with his challenge:

> I have nothing to offer but blood, toil, tears, and sweat. . . . You ask, what is our policy? I will say: It is to wage war by land, sea, and air. War with all our might and with all the strength God has given us. (Quoted in *Classic Speeches*, Richard Crosscup, Philosophical Library, p. 77)

Winston Churchill had a passion for victory.

There is, however, another war raging today. It is the battle for the souls of men; it is a battle between the forces of light and darkness. It is a battle between the armies of God and Satan, resulting in eternal life to those who believe and eternal death to the unbelieving.

When I speak of the "soul," I speak of the "real you." Genesis 2:7 states, "God . . . breathed into his nostrils the breath of life, and the man became a living being."

Scripture tells us that the soul is of infinite value. Jesus asked, "What good will it be for a man if he gains the whole world, yet forfeits his soul? Or what can man give in exchange for his soul?" (Matt. 16:26) To lose one's soul is the loss of all losses.

For the souls of mankind, Jesus was born. He lived and died with the souls of the world in view. No expenditure is too great if by making that expenditure a soul is won. No sacrifice is too deep if by sacrificing a soul is won. No trip is too far if by taking that trip a soul is won. No suffering is too intense if by suffering a soul is won. The soul is of indescribable worth.

The word *passion* also needs to be explored. "Passion" means more than desire. It speaks of a commitment so complete that it is willing to sacrifice. It speaks of a "suffering love." The work of Christ on the cross is often referred to as His "passion." Jesus, you will remember, "set his face toward Jerusalem" with a single-mindedness that was total. The word *passion* involves an identification with the eternal destiny of others.

A SINGLE PASSION

As a boy, I was the proud owner of an attractive pocket knife. The knife had three blades, a can opener, screw driver, and nail file, plus a minature pair of scissors. The whole knife cost a dollar but wasn't worth a dime. The problem was that the knife was too versatile. It did many things poorly but nothing well.

Single-mindedness for a lifetime usually makes the difference between success and failure. Jesus said, "If your eyes are good, your whole body will be full of light" (Matt. 6:22). In essence, Jesus said, "Be a single-eyed person."

James reminds us that "a double-minded person [is] unstable in all he does" (James 1:8). The double-minded are like the waves of the sea, blown and scattered by the wind.

I once heard of a mule who starved to death between two stacks of hay simply because he couldn't decide from which stack to eat! Double-mindedness results in confusion and instability.

The life of Jesus illustrates a single passion. Luke tells us, "The son of Man came to seek and to save what was lost" (19:10). To seek and to save the lost was Jesus' passion.

Satan continually tried to detour Jesus. In the wilderness temptation, Satan offered, "All this I will give You, if You will bow down and worship me" (Matt. 4:9) Satan really said, here's a short cut. Forget the cross and I'll give you "the kingdoms of the world" *now* — in a hurry.

Jesus recognized Satan's voice and refused his offer.

When Jesus was dying, Satan spoke through the religious leaders' taunting, "Come down now from the cross, and we will believe You" (see Matt. 27:42). Jesus refused! After having vinegar put to His mouth, Jesus called out, "It is finished." With that He bowed His head and gave up His life (John 19:30). The passion of Jesus was awe inspiring.

The life of the Apostle Paul also demonstrated a single passion. He knew who he was, and what God had called him to do. To the Romans, he wrote, "Paul, a servant of Christ Jesus, called to be an apostle and set apart for the gospel of God" (Rom. 1:1)

To the Corinthians he said, "Paul, called to be an apostle of Christ Jesus by the will of God" (1 Cor. 1:1).

Listen to his words to the churches of Galatia: "Paul, an apostle — sent not from men nor by men, but by Jesus Christ and God the Father . . ." (Gal. 1:1).

So that no one would miss his *single* passion, Paul said, "This one thing I do: Forgetting what is behind and straining toward what is ahead, I press on toward the goal to win the prize for which God has called me heavenward in Christ Jesus" (Phil. 3:13-14). Nothing could deflect the passion of his calling.

The famous Dutch artist Vincent Van Gogh at one point in life felt called to be an evangelist. He was raised in a Christian home. His father served as a pastor. At the age of twenty-four, in 1878, he enrolled in a school for evangelism in Brussels. After graduating, he preached for a year. Then for reasons unknown to us, Vincent Van Gogh forsook his call.

In 1889 he began to paint as a driven man, finishing 200 paintings in two years time. Then at age thirty-seven, confused and sick of life, with a borrowed gun, he ended his life. How tragic!

Paul urged Timothy, "Fan into flame the gift of God, which is in you" (2 Tim. 1:6). He seemed to say, "Timothy, fight the fading flame. Tend your gifts! Cultivate a single passion for the souls of men."

A HEART PASSION

Pastor John Henry Jowett has given us some searching words about a heart passion:

> The gospel of a broken heart demands the ministry of bleeding hearts. . . . As soon as we cease to bleed, we cease to bless. . . . We can never heal the needs we do not feel. Tearless hearts can never be the heralds of His passion *The Passion for Souls*, Fleming H. Revell, pp. 30, 34).

By a heart passion, I mean a *caring, identifying* concern.

At times the great missionary David Livingston could not speak the language of the people he met, but all *felt* his caring passion.

Abraham of the Old Testament had a heart passion (Genesis 18). As he faced the people of Sodom, he was compelled to intercede with God on their behalf. "Will you sweep away the righteous with the wicked? What if there are fifty righteous people in the city? Will you really sweep away and not spare the place for the sake of the fifty righteous people that are in it?" (Gen. 18:23-24)

Because Abraham could not find fifty righteous people, he asked the Lord to withhold judgment for the sake of forty-five, then forty, then thirty, twenty; and finally he pleaded for the sake of ten. Abraham probably thought, *If my nephew Lot, and his wife, and their children, along with their mates could be counted as righteous, I'll have my ten, and God will spare all the people of Sodom.* However, not even ten righteous could be found!

Moses also had a heart passion. While Moses was on Mt. Sinai, the Children of Israel made a golden calf and danced around it, and Moses reacted with great distress and anguish. Moses prayed: "These people . . . have made themselves gods of gold. But now, please forgive their sin—but if not, then blot me out of the book You have written" (Ex. 32:31-32).

Moses identified with his people so completely that he was willing to be blotted out of God's book forever. That's a heart passion!

The life of Jesus illustrates a heart passion. Once He looked over His beloved city Jerusalem and wept because of their seeming indifference. "O Jerusalem, Jerusalem . . . how often I longed to gather your children together, as a hen gathers her chicks under her wings, and you were not willing" (Matt. 23:37).

Have you ever felt like that? Have you ever wept concerning an individual, a family, a village, a city, or the world?

Bob Pierce, the founder of World Vision, used to ask, "Is your heart broken by the things that break the heart of God?" I believe he was talking about a heart passion.

A LIFE PASSION

The Apostle Paul also illustrates a life passion. Paul shared the heights and depth of his passion in Romans 9:1-3: "I speak the truth in Christ—I am not lying, my conscience confirms it in the Holy Spirit—I have great sorrow and unceasing anguish in my heart. For I could wish that I myself were cursed and cut off from Christ for the sake of my brothers, those of my own race, the people of Israel."

I believe Paul is saying, "I am willing to go to hell, if by going to hell my loved ones and countrymen will be saved." Paul was captured by an all-controlling, all-consuming life passion.

Recently, I have read articles warning against what we westerners call "burn out"; that is, fatigue that comes from stress and overwork. And I am fully sympathetic with this real possibility. However, there's another side to this issue. We need to remember that some men and women of God in the past not only *burned out* for God; some of them were even *burned up* for God.

To Timothy, Paul said, "I have fought a good fight, I have *finished* my course, I have kept the faith" (2 Tim. 4:7, KJV).

As we live a Spirit-led life—doing what God has called us to do and keeping spiritually renewed—it is unlikely that many of us will burn out. Yet Henry Martyn, missionary to India, prayed, "I desire to burn out for my God."

Hebrews 12:3-4 urges us to consider Jesus and His life passion as an encouragement for us to do the same, and then the writer adds, "You have not yet resisted to the point of shedding your blood."

An illustration of a life passion is seen in the life of Rachel, the wife of Jacob. The crowning glory of a Hebrew woman was to bear a child. Because Rachel was barren her shame and concern deepened into desperation. The Scripture reads, "When Rachel saw that she was not bearing Jacob any children, she became jealous of her sister. So she said to Jacob, 'Give me children, or I'll die!' " (Gen. 30:1) But the Lord was very aware of Rachel's barrenness and gave her a son.

The prayer of John Knox of Scotland reminds me of Rachel's prayer, "Lord, give me Scotland or else I die." In both situations God responded to the prayers of His children.

May we too pray for a passion for souls as we endeavor to witness faithfully.

REMINDERS

● "The gospel of a broken heart demands the ministry of a bleeding heart." (J.H. Jowett)

● "We can never heal the needs we do not feel." (J. H. Jowett)

● "Moses went back unto the Lord and said, "Oh, what a great sin these people have committed! They have made themselves gods of gold. But now, please forgive their sin—but if not, then blot me out of the book You have written" (Ex. 32:31-32).

● "I speak the truth in Christ—I am not lying, my conscience confirms it in the Holy Spirit—I have great sorrow and unceasing anguish in my heart. For I could wish that I myself were cursed and cut off from Christ for the sake of my brothers, those of my own race, the people of Israel" (Rom. 9:1-3).

I am obligated both to Greeks and non-Greeks, both to the wise and the foolish. That is why I am so eager to preach the Gospel also to you who are at Rome.   Romans 1:14–15

Then they said to each other, "We're not doing right. This is a day of good news and we are keeping it to ourselves. If we wait until daylight, punishment will overtake us. Let's go at once and report this to the royal palace."   2 Kings 7:9

People all around you are indeed hungry for the good news that Christ died for their sin. Without Jesus, they have no hope of knowing God or having eternal life.

God opens up unique witnessing opportunities to you, and sometimes in the most unlikely of circumstances. He doesn't expect eloquence, but He does expect obedience.

You have in your possession the greatest news ever announced. Why be so hesitant to share it with others?

Christ has commanded us, "You are to go into all the world, to preach the Good News to everyone, everywhere." If we love Him, we will obey Him: "The one who obeys Me is the one who loves Me."

Whenever you're alone with someone for a few minutes or more, consider it a divine appointment.

> Bill Bright (*Witnessing without Fear*, Tyndale, pp. 50–51)

FOUR
Compelling Reasons for Witnessing

When David Ben Gurion, the first prime minister of the state of Israel, was asked what it would take to establish his new nation, he threw back his head and laughed. "All I need starts with the letter A — *a* lot of planes, *a* lot of guns, *a* lot of money, and *a* lot of men," he responded.

We too could say that all we need to share our faith starts with the letter A — *a* lot of love, *a* lot of faith, *a* lot of courage, and *a* lot of wisdom.

FOUR COMPELLING REASONS TO WITNESS

Witnessing is not something that comes naturally to most of us. And yet there are solid biblical reasons why we must witness. Let me list four compelling reasons.

1. *My knowledge makes me responsible.* I remember when Dr. Jonas Salk discovered the final phases of the polio vaccine. At last there was a cure to free the thousands of people suffering from the crippling disease of polio. But just suppose Dr. Salk had decided to withhold that life-saving vaccine. Such action would be uncaring, if not criminal.

In like manner, each believer has the cure for the fatal affliction of sin. We have the chance to make a lasting difference in
the lives of others.

Writing to the congregation in Rome, Paul shares his personal responsibility. "I am obligated both to Greeks and non-
Greeks, both to the wise and the foolish. That is why I am so
eager to preach the Gospel also to you who are at Rome"
(Romans. 1:14-15). The weight of this debt drove Paul relent-
lessly for a lifetime.

Contrary to the view of some, the world doesn't owe any of us
anything. Rather we as believers owe the world a caring, intelligent telling of "God's Good News." Simply put, *To know is to
owe*. Our knowledge makes us responsible.

2. *My blessings make me responsible.* To possess God's salvation
imposes responsiblity. *To have, means to owe.* The intriguing
story in 2 Kings 7:3-9 of four starving lepers outside the gates of
Samaria illustrates this truth. Their situation was desperate. As
lepers, they were forbidden to enter the city, and yet if they
didn't get food, they would die of starvation. They decided to
throw themselves upon the mercy of the Syrians. However,
upon entering the camp, they found it deserted! The Scripture
tells us, "The Lord made the host of the Syrians to hear a noise
of a great host. . . . Therefore they rose and fled in the twi-
light. . . . And when these lepers came to the uttermost part of
the camp, they went into one tent, and did eat and drink. . . .
Then they said one to another, 'We do not well; this day is a
day of good tidings, and we hold our peace' " (vv. 6-9, KJV).

Once these four lepers had eaten they were smitten with
concern for those who were still starving. They confessed that
they had good news and were obligated to share it with others.

This powerful truth applies to each person who possesses
salvation and for one reason or other neglects to witness. Frankly, I believe it is sinful to be silent when we possess the Good

News. Our blessings make us responsible.

The Old Testament Prophet Ezekiel points out the issue of human responsibility: "When I say to the wicked, 'O wicked man, you will surely die,' and you do not speak out to dissuade him from his ways, that wicked man will die for his sin, and I will hold you accountable for his blood. But if you do warn the wicked man to turn from his ways and he does not do so, he will die for his sin, but you will have saved yourself" (Ezek. 33:8-9).

Ezekiel discharged his responsibility by speaking out. This passage teaches that failure to sound the warning incurs individual responsibility.

Jesus' story of the Good Samaritan in Luke 10:30-36 also teaches responsibility. The priest and the Levite saw the desperate condition of the beaten traveler, but passed by and did nothing. Their sin was their failure to do something for the beaten man. Their blessings made them responsible.

In the Parable of the Talents (Matt. 25:14-30), the worker with one talent was condemned because he buried his talent and did nothing to use it. He was accused of being both wicked and lazy (v. 26). The parable emphasizes that our many blessings make us responsible. *To have is to owe!*

3. *The Great Commission makes me responsible.* After the ascension of Jesus, His disciples were anxious to know when Jesus would set up His kingdom. Jesus told them, "It is not for you to know the times or dates the Father has set by His own authority" (Acts 1:7). After telling them that they were *not* to know when, He outlined exactly what they were to know. "You will receive power when the Holy Spirit comes on you; and you will be My witnesses in Jerusalem, and in all Judea and Samaria, and to the ends of the earth" (Acts 1:8). The commission of Jesus is so clear that no Christian can claim ignorance. Jesus stated, "You will be My witnesses."

After reading Matthew 28:19-20, Pastor William Carey of England was deeply concerned for the people of India. He thought, "Does this commission of Jesus apply to me? Does God really want me to go as His representative to share the Good News?" Carey decided to speak about this matter in a gathering of the local association of ministers. The presiding pastor bluntly rebuked young Carey and informed him that when God wanted to save the heathen, He would do it without his help. However, in spite of this rebuke, William Carey responded to the commission given by Jesus. He and his family accepted their responsibility to share the Good News and became missionaries to India; and consequently, William Carey became the father of the modern missionary movement.

George Whitefield, challenged by the Great Commission, crossed the Atlantic Ocean thirteen times to reach the people of the American colonies, and that was at a time when it took three months to cross the Atlantic Ocean in a sailing ship. Whitefield preached three and four times a day for thirty-three years. He had a specific burden for the people of the American colonies. He died at age fifty-five.

Much as God the Father sent Jesus into the world, God the Son is sending people today (John 20:21). Well, how did the Father send Jesus? He became one of us. The Word became flesh (John 1:14). And that is still God's approach. He uses ordinary people like you and me. The commission of Jesus makes each believer responsible to share the Good News.

4. *My position makes me responsible.* The Apostle Paul was sensitive regarding his position as a believer in Christ. He said, "We are therefore Christ's ambassadors, as though God were making His appeal through us. We implore you on Christ's behalf: Be reconciled to God" (2 Cor. 5:20).

It is sobering to realize that Almighty God makes His appeal to people through you and me. Charles B. Williams in his *New Testament in the Language of the People* (Moody Press) translates 2 Corinthians 5:20 powerfully, "So I am an envoy to represent Christ, because it is through me that God is making His appeal.

As one representing Christ, I beg you, be reconciled to God."

That awesome position implies responsibility. Each and every believer is either a good ambassador or a poor ambassador, but we cannot escape being an ambassador. In the light of our calling, we must share the Good News.

John Currier, a man who could not read or write, was found guilty of murder and sentenced to prison for life in 1949. Later he was transferred from prison and paroled to work for a wealthy farmer near Nashville, Tennessee.

In 1968, however, his sentence was terminated. State Correction Department records show that a letter was written to the convict and the farmer for whom he worked. The letter said he was free.

But Currier never saw the letter or even knew it had been written. One year went by, then two, then five, and finally, ten; and still he did not know that he was free.

By this time, the farmer to whom he had been paroled was dead, but Currier kept working, serving out his sentence. He was given a little money for personal needs—five dollars a week at first, then a little more, and finally twenty dollars weekly.

But life was hard and filled with labor. He slept in a drafty trailer, taking baths in a horse trough with a garden hose. Life held very little joy and no promise.

This went on till 1978. Then a state parole officer learned of his plight and told him of the missing letter. Carrier sued the State of Tennessee for $600,000. Some thought the sum was too small.

Would it matter to you if someone sent you an important message—the most important of your life, and year after year the urgent message was never delivered.

But think of a different situation. A child is born, grows up, and dies without once hearing there is a God who loves him. He is never told that the God who made him sent His Son to deliver him from sin and give him everlasting life.

He lives in servitude to a cruel and powerful master, Satan. And when he has his children, they too are born to live and die in bondage.

This is the condition of all those who live outside the circle of the family of God. Our *position* as an ambassador makes us responsible to witness.

Why should you as a believer witness? Consider these eight biblical reasons:

1. Your knowledge makes you responsible (Rom. 1:14-16).
2. Your blessings make you responsible (2 Kings 7:3-9).
3. The Great Commission makes you responsible (Matt. 28:19-20).
4. Your position in Christ makes you responsible (2 Cor. 5:20).
5. The constraining love of Christ (2 Cor. 5:14).
6. The judgment of each believer (2 Cor. 5:10).
7. The terror of the Lord (2 Cor. 5:11).
8. The costly work of Christ (2 Cor. 5:15).

Why should we witness? Because Jesus said so, and that's *reason enough!*

The story is told of a severe shortage of currency in Great Britain during the rule of Oliver Cromwell. Representatives carefully searched the empire in the hopes of finding silver to meet the emergency. After several months, a committee returned to Cromwell with its findings. "We have searched the empire in vain to find silver. To our dismay, we found none except in the great cathedrals, where the saints are constructed of choice silver."

To this, Cromwell responded, "Let's melt down the saints, and put them into circulation." That's our need today!

REMINDERS
- All believers have a debt, simply because they possess God's salvation.
- To rattle off Bible verses mechanically, with the hope of somehow discharging our spiritual responsibility, is a farce.
- It is a sin to be silent.
- The Great Commission is so plain that no earnest believer can claim ignorance.
- Each Christian is either a good ambassador or a bad ambassador, but we can't escape *being* an ambassador.

Jesus came to us as the first whole person since Adam and Eve before the Fall. It is Jesus, then, who provides for us the model of what it means to be human. By following His lead we will not only become more like God Himself but we will find ourselves becoming more comfortable with our humanity and with evangelism which will begin to flow naturally from who we are.

Rebecca Pippert (*Out of the Salt Shaker*, InterVarsity Press, p. 33)

Sometimes the question is asked, "Which is more important in witnessing, the life I live or the words I say?" This question throws the consistency of our lives and our verbal witness into a false antithesis. It's like asking which wing of an airplane is more important, the right or the left! Obviously both are essential, and you don't have anything without both. Life and lip are inseparable in an effective witness to Christ.

Paul Little (*How to Give Away Your Faith*, InterVarsity Press, p. 35)

FIVE

Jesus, the Faithful Witness

J esus was the most attractive witness who ever lived! He loved people intensely and wasn't afraid to show it. At a wedding party in Cana, He performed the first of His miracles, in all probability, to avoid embarrassment to the bride and groom because the refreshments had run out. For the most part, people wanted to have Jesus around. Even the children flocked to Him. Prejudice wasn't a part of His nature. Freely and naturally, He witnessed to rich Nicodemus, self-righteous Zaccheus, and even the Samaritan woman who had been married five times. Jesus, without a doubt, is the incomparable witness. Twice, the Bible calls Him "the faithful witness" (Rev. 1:5; 3:14).

A DIVINE COMPULSION

John 4 shows us, step by step, how Jesus witnessed faithfully. The passage pictures Jesus and His disciples traveling from Judea to Galilee. Contrary to the usual custom, they traveled through the land of Samaria. John calls attention to that fact, saying that Jesus "had to go through Samaria" (John 4:4). But why did He have to go through Samaria? Certainly there were other roads on which He and His disciples could have traveled. In fact, orthodox Jews avoided Samaritans like a plague. To avoid Samaria, they took the long road across the Jordan River through Peraea and then back into Galilee to make sure they did not travel through the land of the Samaritans. The Jews looked with scorn on all Samaritans because they viewed them as a race of half-breeds.

So why did Jesus travel through Samaria? Jesus made a special point of journeying through Samaria for the single purpose of speaking to a certain Samaritan woman.

The *King James Version* uses the word *must* in John 4:4 — "must needs go through Samaria." Jesus was irresistably drawn to go through Samaria. The word *must* is used in the way of saying that "a triangle must have three sides." *Must* conveys Christ's intention to meet and win the Samaritan woman's heart. The word *must* shines with the glow of God's sovereignty and purpose. And this divine compulsion is a key to witnessing faithfully. Each witness should understand and feel something of God's compulsion.

It is interesting to notice that Jesus did not begin witnessing by asking this woman hard, confusing, theological questions. Rather, Jesus began by attempting to meet her need for water. Then, simply and gently, He led her step by step to focus on her spiritual need, and we must do the same.

PEOPLE ARE THIRSTY

What do we know about this Samaritan woman? We know that she was thirsty. John tells us it was "about the sixth hour" (John 4:6), or just about noontime that they met. At midday it is uncomfortably hot in Samaria, and this woman had come to draw cool drinking water from the well on the outskirts of the city of Sychar.

In John 3 Jesus talked with a man—Nicodemus, the leader of

the Jews. In chapter 4 He now witnesses to a woman of Samaria. What a contrast in those two! Nicodemus was a Jew, and this woman was a Samaritan. Nicodemus was a brilliant scholar, and she was probably of average intelligence. Nicodemus was a moral, respected leader. The woman at the well was immoral and currently living with a man who was not her husband. Nicodemus had gone to Jesus, whereas Jesus went to the woman.

Yet underneath these external differences both of these individuals were thirsty and in need of living water. In reality, all mankind is on a never ending quest for satisfaction and completeness. We drink only to thirst again.

Not only do we know that this woman was thirsty, but we also know that she was in a certain sense a religious seeker.

Whether we acknowledge it or not, most people are religious. This woman knew all about the religious heritage of the Jews (v. 12), and she was even expecting the Messiah to come (v. 25). Possibly she secretly longed for personal liberation from her enslaving habits.

She also was aware of the religious controversy that raged in that day. In fact, verse 20 shows that she was ready to argue the validity of Mt. Gerizim versus Jerusalem as the right place to worship. She no doubt had awareness of the Old Testament and some of its teachings.

But in spite of all her religious knowledge, she was empty-hearted. It is encouraging to know that no matter who we are, no matter what the nature of our emptiness is, Jesus is adequate to meet our need. Christ is the answer to all the situations of life! He alone is able to quench that deep thirst within. Jesus knew all about this woman just as He knows all about each one of us. Everything is an open book to Him.

FOUR PRINCIPLES OF WITNESSING USED BY JESUS

1. *Jesus asked a favor.* Jesus did not start witnessing to the Samaritan woman by telling her that she was a wicked woman of

the street. The kindness of Jesus is seen in a sensitive approach to her. "Will you give me a drink?" He asked (v. 7). The best way to win someone's confidence is to ask a simple favor. Kindness often penetrates the most complex personality. He did not say, "Lady, do you know who I am?" No, He began at a point of common interest—their mutual need for water. By a series of questions Jesus eventually got to her heart.

The first step in witnessing faithfully is to gain the interest and attention of those to whom we witness. At times, I have watched some people dive in, rattling off verses and not even taking the time to introduce themselves, let alone carry on a normal conversation. Our approach at times can be crude, because we fail to establish a common, thoughtful, courteous point of interest. How did Jesus begin? He began by gently asking a simple favor. Rule one, ask a favor.

2. *Jesus refused to argue.* When Jesus asked for water, the woman answered, "You are a Jew and I am a Samaritan woman. How can You ask me for a drink?" (John 4:9) She immediately raised the question of *racial prejudice.* "Why are you talking with me when You should hate me?" she seemed to say.

But Jesus refused to be drawn into an argument. Attitudes of racial discrimination are wrong, and therefore He did not debate with the woman. Rather, Jesus demonstrated in a practical way that He sincerely cared for her as a person. Prejudice was unknown to Jesus.

At times in our witness we get caught up in heated arguments that usually do more harm than good. Remember, "A man convinced against his will is of the same opinion still." It is possible to win the argument and lose the person. The Apostle James reminds Christians to be "quick to listen, slow to speak, and slow to become angry" (1:19). Nothing profitable is accomplished when we try to force people to acknowledge Christ. Jesus didn't argue. We are to contend for the faith, but we're not to be contentious. Rule two, refuse to argue.

3. *Jesus aroused her interest.* John 4:10 says, "Jesus answered her, 'If you knew the gift of God and who it is that asks you for a drink, you would have asked Him and He would have given you living water.' " He seemed to say teasingly, "I know something you don't know." The fact that He knew something she did not know aroused her curiosity.

That certainly does not mean that we must do strange things to gain attention. At times some people will think we're odd enough, but that does not give us the excuse to be foolish in our conduct or our methods. Paul Little wrote, "Oddballism may momentarily arouse curiosity about us, but it tends to discourage true interest in the Gospel" (*How to Give Away Your Faith*, InterVarsity Press, p. 34).

I have found that a helpful way to arouse genuine interest is simply to ask a person, "By the way, are you interested in spiritual things?" If he says yes, I proceed by sharing what Jesus Christ means to me. If he says no, I ask, "What do you think it means to be a Christian?" Often those two questions will open the door to witness faithfully. Jesus aroused the interest of the Samaritan woman. Rule three, arouse interest.

4. *Jesus awakened her conscience.* To be effective witnesses we may wisely probe the area of need. Jesus got to the heart of the matter. In verse 16 He said to the woman, "Go, call your husband and come back." Outwardly, that seemed like an innocent request. But actually it dug deep into her past failure. She answered, " 'I have no husband.' . . . Jesus said to her, 'You are right when you say you have no husband. The fact is, you have had five husbands, and the man you now have is not your husband. What you have just said is quite true.' 'Sir,' the woman said, 'I can see that You are a prophet.' " (John 4:17-19).

What the woman really was saying was, "You are right, Jesus, I need help. I'm thirsty." Jesus awakened her conscience. He spoke to her point of weakness, and she saw herself for what she really was—a sinful, frustrated person, needing salvation. Rule four, awaken people to their need.

It is interesting and exciting to see the change in this woman's thinking as the conversation with Jesus evolved. In verse 9 she called Him a Jew—just a traveler. In verse 12, she suggested that possibly He might be "greater than Jacob." In verse 19 she called Him "a prophet," and in verse 29 she called Him "the Messiah."

What an attractive and powerful example of witnessing this is. The woman's conversation with Jesus was so life-changing that she forgot her water pots and hurried off to the city to tell her friends all about Jesus. She was changed from a harlot to a herald of the Good News.

One of the many lessons in John 4 is the importance of learning the true needs of those to whom we witness. If we sincerely care for people, usually they will sense our concern, and in all probability, give us a fair hearing.

The woman of Samaria met Jesus and Jesus satisfied her needs. She came to the well, seeking water to quench her physical thirst, and she went away with the water of eternal life, never to thirst again.

This woman's life was so dramatically changed that her friends couldn't wait to see for themselves what had happened to her. "Many of the Samaritans from that town believed in Him because of the woman's testimony, 'He told me everything I ever did'" (John 4:39). They also came to Jesus and believed and experienced salvation. No witness can do better than copy Jesus, the true and "faithful witness."

REMINDERS
● Witnessing goes beyond what we say, to what we really are and what we do.
● "There is a God-shaped vacuum in every heart" (Blaise Pascal).
● The first rule in faithful witnessing is to gain the interest and

attention of those to whom we witness.
● "A man convinced against his will is of the same opinion still."
● "Oddballism may momentarily arouse curiosity about us, but it tends to discourage true interest in the Gospel" (Paul Little).

Our problem in evangelism is not that we don't have enough information — it is that we don't know how to be ourselves. We forget we are called to be witnesses to what we have seen and know, not to what we don't know. The key is authenticity and *obedience,* not a doctorate in theology. We haven't grasped that it really is okay for us to be who we are, when we are with non-Christians, even if we don't have all the answers to their questions or if our knowledge of Scripture is limited.

Rebecca Pippert (*Out of the Salt Shaker,* InterVarsity Press, p. 24)

The real question is not, "Is this the best time for a personal word for Christ?" but it is "Am I willing to improve this time for Christ, and for a precious soul, whether it is the best time or not?" If the Christian waits until the sinner gives sign of a desire for help, or until the Christian thinks that a loving word to the sinner will be most timely, he is not likely to begin at all. The only safe rule for his guidance — if indeed a Christian needs a specific rule as a guide — is to speak lovingly of Christ and of Christ's love for the individual whenever one has an opportunity of choosing his subject of conversation in an interview with an individual who may be in special need, yet who has given no special indication of it.

Henry Clay Trumbull (*Taking Men Alive,* C.G. Trumbull, Fleming H. Revell, p. 52)

SIX

Five Marks of the Faithful Witness

S ome Christians suffer from spiritual lockjaw. This affliction is found among believers of all ages, so that a large
number have never told anyone who Jesus is, or what
He has done in their lives. The root cause of this silence appears
to be fear of failure.

FIVE CHARACTERISTICS OF THE FAITHFUL WITNESS

Philip, the layman, provides a step by step example for us to
follow. Five characteristics of the faithful witness appear in Acts
8:26-40.

1. *The faithful witness desires to obey God.* Philip, a Greek-
speaking Jew, was selected as a deacon in the original church
(Acts 6:5). As he faithfully served the church as a deacon, his
ministry expanded to that of an evangelist. He appears to be one
of the first to go outside the circle of Judaism to share the
Gospel in Samaria.

The response to Philip's witnessing was so dramatic that
"when the crowds heard Philip and saw the miraculous signs he
did, they all paid close attention to what he said" (Acts 8:6),

and "there was great joy in that city" (v. 8). Philip experienced the kind of response that most of us dream about — an attentive audience, breathtaking miracles, and great joy.

At the peak of success, the Lord told him to leave it all and travel to Gaza, a desert place eighty miles south. Common sense protested, but the voice of God was unmistakably clear. God led Philip from the city to the desert, from crowds to a particular man, from success to the unknown.

Here's a basic lesson for each of us — God's ways are not man's ways. Had Philip listed all the reasons for going or staying, he would have stayed in Samaria. Philip's obedience is *the key* to God's blessing upon his life. We too need to be quick to hear the voice of God.

Philip obeyed (v. 27). He didn't discuss, debate, or delay; he simply obeyed.

During a tense period in World War II, the North African campaign bogged down largely because the enlisted men lost confidence in their officers. The poor morale resulted in a half-heartedness that nearly caused disaster. In the same way, a loss of confidence in God's authority spells defeat. God calls each of us to the discipline of obedience.

We've all seen the bumper sticker, "Honk, if you love Jesus." Frankly, I'm not a bumper sticker person, but if I were, I would prefer to forget the "honking" and have a sticker reading, "Obey, if you love Jesus."

Philip's immediate obedience reminds me of Abraham. God called Abraham to do a humanly impossible thing. He commanded, "Take your son, your only son, Isaac, whom you love. . . . Sacrifice him there as a burnt offering on one of the mountains I will tell you about" (Gen. 22:2). That command was contrary to all that God had promised Abraham. Isaac was a miracle son. Through Isaac and his descendants, God's promises to Israel would be fulfilled. Yet, in spite of all that, Abraham didn't hesitate, but "rose up early" to obey God.

Once we agree to obey the Lord, all the other steps are easier. The best way to see farther ahead in God's plan is to go as far ahead as you can see. Faithfulness today prepares you for tomorrow.

2. *The faithful witness recognizes that the Gospel is for all people.* As Philip traveled to Gaza, he met a caravan of soldiers and merchants, and in the center, a celebrity—the treasurer of Ethiopia. This was the person to whom Philip was sent, but . . . who was this man?

He was probably a Gentile. We're told that this Ethiopian had just been to Jerusalem to worship. Some have suggested that he may have been a Jew who had reached a high position in the government of Ethiopia, like Joseph, who ruled Egypt, or Daniel, who reached a high position in Babylon. Both are illustrations of Jews who prospered in Gentile nations. However, most Bible scholars believe that this man was a Gentile who had been won over to Judaism. The Good News is for both Jews and Gentiles.

He was probably a member of the black race. Each witness must be fully persuaded that in Jesus Christ there is neither Jew nor Greek, bond nor free, male nor female. Regardless of origin, or status, or color, all people are equally loved by God and are made in His image. The inclusive Gospel cannot be shared by exclusive people. The love of God is color blind. To label any person as worthy or unworthy is inconsistent with God's mercy and grace.

He was a man of great authority. The person to whom Philip was sent was a person of significant influence. Specifically, he was in charge of the government's money and served as secretary of the treasury of Ethiopia.

The Good News is not only for all races, but for all levels of society. It is for both the poor and the rich, the up and out, as well as the down and out.

D.L. Moody, the founder of Moody Bible Institute, had a deep concern for the poor and the oppressed. The then mayor of

Chicago, "Long John" Wentworth, secured the North Market Hall for Moody's Sunday School because he saw this as a hand of help to the restless and underprivileged poor of the city.

Even today at Moody Bible Institute, 2,000 students reach out through scores of ministries to bring the Gospel to the forgotten poor. But that is only a part of our mission field. Periodically, we attempt to wisely present a clear witness to the leaders of our city, state, and the nation, because the Good News is for all men and women.

He was religious. Scripture tells us that the Ethiopian "had gone to Jerusalem to worship" (Acts 8:27). This man recognized that he had a personal need and exerted a great effort to meet those spiritual needs. He was a seeker of truth, and Philip met him as he was reading the Old Testament account from Isaiah 53.

The Gospel is for the whole world—Jew and Gentile, black, red, yellow, and white, celebrity and common folk, religious or otherwise. Philip the layman recognized that the Gospel is for *all* people.

3. *The faithful witness needs a sense of urgency.* Acts 8:30 reads, "Then Philip *ran* up to the chariot." A fire burned inside Philip. He appears to be Spirit-filled and Spirit-led. Urgency gripped him.

President Abraham Lincoln is reported to have said, "I like to see a person preach and teach like he's fighting bees." Apparently, Lincoln appreciated enthusiasm. The word *enthusiasm* is a good word that belongs to the Christian church. The root of the word comes from the Greek *theos* meaning "God," and the prefix *en,* meaning "to be filled." The idea of the word is "to be filled with God." Of all people, Christians ought to be the most enthusiastic people in the entire world.

The early apostolic Christians revealed that kind of charisma, "praising God and enjoying the favor of all the people" (Acts 2:47). Their favor was directly related to their attractiveness and their attractiveness grew out of their joy and enthusiasm. The psalmist reminds us, "It is fitting for the upright to praise Him" (Ps. 33:1).

Commenting on the enthusiasm of the early Christians, an English bishop remarked, "Wherever Paul preached he either had a revival or a riot, but wherever I preach, they usually serve tea." Like Paul, Philip was filled with God, and this revealed itself in a sense of warmth and urgency. We will consider more about this urgency in chapter 14.

4. *The faithful witness knows the Scriptures.* Running up to the chariot, Philip heard the man reading Isaiah the prophet. " 'Do you understand what you are reading?' Philip asked" (Acts 8:30).

Notice how God sovereignly worked to pinpoint the Ethiopian's spiritual need. He was reading from Isaiah 53. He had been to Jerusalem and was returning, evidently spiritually empty. He was searching that great messianic passage in Isaiah but could not understand its meaning.

Had Philip not responded to the Holy Spirit as he did, this man would have returned home empty and ignorant. He would not have known the forgiveness available in Jesus Christ. Philip immediately entered into the Ethiopian's experience at the critical point of his need. The man was reading the passage, "He was led as a sheep to the slaughter . . ." And to answer the question, "Who is the prophet talking about?" Philip "began with that very passage of Scripture and told him the Good News about Jesus" (Acts 8:35).

It is important to relate directly to a person's need, to be so familiar with Scripture and the need of the person witnessed to, that we can wisely make the proper application. Coming to know the Scriptures calls for a serious commitment as well as time. However, each of us have to begin where we are, with what we know, as we develop expertise.

We can learn four helpful principles from Philip's actions.

First, Philip "opened his mouth." Occasionally, some people say that they are unable to verbalize the plan of salvation, that *they witness by their lives.* The witness of our daily life is first and foremost. In fact, if we do not live the Gospel, we shouldn't share it. This is one of the mega stumbling stones of present-day Christianity. And yet, it is imperative that we articulate the Good News.

I can live my Christian life forever, and that alone is not sufficient to bring anyone to saving faith. The Gospel must be verbalized. We need to open our mouths. The psalmist proclaimed, "Let the redeemed of the Lord say so" (Ps. 107:2, KJV). The biblical ideal is an authentic life coupled with dedicated lips, sharing the Good News.

Second, Philip *began.* Often we feel the urge to begin. We promise the Lord in those special moments of life to begin to witness, but for one reason or other we fail to start. Philip opened his mouth . . . and *began.*

Third, Philip began with the very passage of Scripture the man was reading. Isaiah 53 as quoted in Acts 8:32-33 graphically speaks of the sufferings of Jesus the Messiah. "He was led like a sheep to the slaughter, and as a sheep before her shearers is silent . . . His life was taken from the earth." The Ethiopian asked who the prophet was talking about (v. 34). Philip then identified Jesus as God's sinless lamb, who alone can forgive our sins. Philip was so familiar with the Scriptures that he was able to make the right application.

Fourth, Philip "told him the good news about Jesus" (v. 35). It is essential in all witnessing to get to Jesus. Not all *about* Jesus, but Jesus and His saving work for sinners.

I am sure that many questions were asked and answered. Evidently, Philip took this man through the entire Gospel. I believe he told the Ethiopian of Jesus' birth, His sinless life, His teaching, His suffering, and His death for all. He must have told the Ethiopian of the resurrection of Jesus, the Great Commission, and of the importance of confessing Christ publicly. Notice, the Ethiopian was ready to make a confession of faith.

5. *The faithful witness seeks decisions.* As they approached a body of water, the Ethiopian asked, "Look, here is water. Why shouldn't I be baptized?" (Acts 8:36). How did he know about baptism? Evidently, Philip had presented the Gospel so completely and convincingly that the Ethiopian was prepared to believe and be baptized. Philip answered, " 'If you believe with all your heart, you may.' The official answered, 'I believe that Jesus Christ is the Son of God' " (Acts 8:37). Upon hearing his confession, Philip baptized this new believer.

On Sunday, October 8, 1871, young D.L. Moody was preaching at Farwell Hall in Chicago on the topic, "What will you do with Jesus?" As he closed the service, he urged his audience to think about a decision and then decide the next Sunday. Soloist Ira Sankey began to sing "Today the Saviour Calls." Even as he sang the song, the fire bells could be heard. The air was heavy with the smell of burning wood because Chicago was on fire. By midnight most of the city was engulfed in flames. Farwell Hall and Moody's home burned to the ground. That specific audience never gathered again. Moody often confessed "that was the worst mistake I ever made." From that night on he vowed whether talking to one person or to thousands, he would press for a decision.

Philip had witnessed faithfully. The Ethiopian was transformed by the power of the Gospel. A new light was on his face and a new thrill in his spirit. He was mastered by a new love — the love of Jesus Christ. Philip, the layman, had faithfully witnessed concerning Jesus Christ, and a soul had been born again.

Philip's experience in witnessing gives us five important principles to practice:

1. *Obey* the voice of God.
2. Recognize that the Gospel is for *everyone*.

3. Share the Good News with *enthusiasm* and urgency.
4. *Know* the Scriptures.
5. *Seek* a decision.

Philip was in a hurry to obey the Lord.

REMINDERS

● First, second, last, and always, the witness must be obedient to the voice of God.

● Faithfulness today will automatically prepare you for what God has for you tomorrow.

● Always remember that the inclusive Gospel cannot be shared by exclusive people.

● Abraham Lincoln said, "I like to see a person preach and teach like he's fighting bees."

● Too many of us are so tactful that we don't make contact.

If a man cleanses himself . . . ,he will be an instrument for
noble purposes, made holy, useful to the Master and prepared to do any good work.

2 Timothy 2:21

Consider the ministry of our Lord Jesus Himself. He was a
man who constantly answered questions. But someone will
say, "Didn't He say that to be saved you have to be as a little
child?" Of course, He did. But did you ever see a little child
who didn't ask questions?

Christianity demands that we have enough compassion to
learn the questions of our generation.

Francis Schaeffer (at an International
Congress on World Evangelization)

SEVEN

Preparing to Witness

A dequate preparation is the secret of feeling at ease in most situations in life. Whether we entertain for dinner, deliver a speech, or share our faith, wise preparation produces a sense of readiness. Let's consider some of the areas of preparation for personal evangelism.

SPIRITUAL PREPARATION

To witness faithfully, we need to have a sure confidence of an intelligent faith in Jesus Christ as God's only provision for our sins.

The assurance of salvation. Jesus said, " 'We speak of what we know, and we testify to what we have seen' " (John 3:11). In other words, we know first hand what we're talking about. A living, personal commitment to Christ is the place to begin. The greater our assurance, the more authentic will be our witness. An uncertain salvation has little appeal. The doubter convinces no one.

Assurance of a personal acceptance by God is not only possible (see 1 John 5:13) but to be desired because it adds credibility to our witnessing. Christian assurance is like a fortress of strength against the attacks of our enemy. An uncertain salvation is disappointing and unattractive, whereas assurance adds enthusiasm and warmth to our sharing.

So, don't waste time in doubt, but rather enjoy your position in Jesus. Assurance is not necessary for salvation, but it is necessary for witnessing effectively.

A consistent Christian life. Although God in His sovereignty can use anything and anyone, He prefers to use dedicated people. The Old Testament tells how God used a lowly donkey to speak His word (Num. 22:21-41), and the New Testament tells us that Peter was rebuked by a crowing bird (Matt. 26:75). Yet, just as a surgeon is careful about the instruments he uses, so is God. A pure heart and clean hands are assets to witnessing.

As growing Christians, we will desire personal holiness while at the same time keeping in touch with our everyday world. There is truth in the old cliche, we can be "so heavenly minded that we are of no earthly good." The call to holiness does not isolate us from the people around us. The Pharisees thought of holiness as a withdrawal from the world in general. However, Jesus illustrated by His life His purity and compassion by identifying with publicans and sinners. He accepted people as they were, while being uncompromising in regard to their sin.

Becky Pippert expressed it this way, "The paradox of agape love is that we accept our neighbor unconditionally and with open arms and at the same time desire moral purity for their lives" *(Out of the Salt Shaker*, InterVarsity Press, p. 90).

God does not require perfect people for witnessing, but He does seek those who are sincerely committed to Him (see Rom. 12:1-2).

A love for people. God loves people and so must we. Jesus continually demonstrated His love for people. His compassion was wide open as He saw hurting people groping in confusion. Jesus said, "As I have loved you, so you must love one another"

(John 13:34). He illustrated that divine love from Bethlehem's manger to Calvary's cross. Jesus loves and cares, and we must do the same.

Our witnessing should really be the overflow of God's love in our lives. To mechanically quote Bible verses with the hope of somehow discharging a spiritual debt is a farce. Love cares *deeply*. Love brings about involvement. Love is felt. God's love in us and reaching out through us is an important key to witnessing faithfully.

Persistent prayer. "Men ought always to pray, and not to faint" (Luke 18:1, KJV). Prayer is God's cure for caving in. We believe greatly in prayer. It is stronger than any and all circumstances.

Before we speak to people about God, it is important that we speak to God about people. God honors prayer. We need to ask the Lord to lead us to the right person, give us the right words, and enable us to make the right application. Prayer is an important step in our spiritual preparation and must precede, accompany, and follow each each witnessing experience.

Perseverance. In the account of the Ethiopian in Acts 8, the Spirit of God told Philip, "Go to that chariot and stay near it" (v. 29). The Greek word for "stay near" often means "glue" or cement together. Go and stick with that person who needs Christ. We need that kind of commitment as we witness faithfully. And yet even that commitment and determination must be balanced by common sense and a heart of love. Remember, our primary responsibility is to "sow the good seed."

Dependence on the Holy Spirit. Before His ascension, Jesus said, "Go and make disciples of all nations, baptizing them in the name of the Father and of the Son and of the Holy Spirit, and teaching them to obey everything I have commanded you. And surely I am with you always, to the very end of the age" (Matt. 28:19-20). That is the amazing and comforting promise of the abiding presence of Jesus with us. Christ indwells every believer through the person of the Holy Spirit. The greater our understanding and reliance on the Holy Spirit, the greater will be our freedom in witnessing. Technically, we may witness to perfection, but only the Holy Spirit can give divine life.

The famous eighteenth-century London preacher, Charles Haddon Spurgeon, commented that a good witness must have holiness of character, spiritual life to a high degree, humility of spirit, a living faith, a thorough earnestness, great simplicity of heart, and a complete surrender to God. Spurgeon had those qualities, and God used him effectively.

MENTAL PREPARATION

Though spiritual preparation is first, God also expects us to prepare our minds. This involves an understanding of the Bible in general, and the Gospel in particular.

Know the Scriptures. The Bible is God's instrument in reaching and changing people. Always remember, the Bible is a sharp, effective weapon. It is called the sword of the Spirit. The more we understand the Bible, the greater will be our confidence. There is no authority that compares with that of the Bible. R.A. Torrey wrote:

A practical knowledge of the Bible involves at least four things:

1. A knowledge of how to use the Bible so as to show men, and make men realize, their need of a Saviour.

2. A knowledge of how to use the Bible so as to show men Jesus as just the Saviour who meets their need.

3. A knowledge of how to use the Bible so as to show men how to make Jesus their own Saviour.

4. A knowledge of how to use the Bible so as to meet the difficulties that stand in the way of men accepting Christ. (*How to Work for Christ*, Revell, p. 25).

A knowledge of the Bible is important to witness faithfully.

Understand the Gospel. Basic as it may seem, an understanding of the Good News is often neglected. To be a faithful witness, one must be able to express in simple words the sinfulness of man, the sinlessness of Jesus, the truth of Christ's sacrificial death for mankind, and God's love to sinners.

Have a right attitude. Some time ago I was flying to a convention in Washington, D.C. A businessman sitting next to me offered me a drink of vodka. In a friendly, natural way I simply answered, "No, thank you."

Sometime later he noticed my Bible and said, "You seem to be religious, and I guess you think I'm an unsavory person."

"No," I replied, "I think you're a very generous person." Immediately, he relaxed and was receptive as I gently shared the Gospel with him.

I could have answered, "No, thank you, I'm a Christian." In all likelihood he would have felt put down, and the door of opportunity would have been harder to open.

We need to be prepared to respond wisely to profanity, off-color stories, drugs, or drinking. Although we may oppose the lifestyle of some to whom we witness, we must always love the individual. Careful mental preparation can avoid land mines. Too often we're caught offguard and respond in such a way as to widen the gap. Paul Little urged preparation for those awkward moments. "Every Christian," he said, "should always have five sure-fire jokes at his disposal. Well chosen, well-timed humor can reset the whole tone of a conversation; it can carry you over a seemingly impossible hurdle. Like remembering names, the only way to remember a joke is to use it immediately after you hear it. If necessary, write it down afterward. Then tell it whenever you get a chance" (*How to Give Away Your Faith*, Inter-Varsity Press, p. 48). There's no doubt about it, a wholesome humorous story can rescue a tense situation.

It is helpful to ask the person to whom you're witnessing for permission to share concerning spiritual things.

Be prepared to use your testimony. Your testimony should be carefully prepared and even memorized so that at a moment's notice you are ready to wisely share the Good News. Whatever you do, be sensitive and tactful.

Tact has been defined as the right touch rather than the wrong touch. Scripture commands us to let our lights shine, but remember, not like a blow torch! J. Oswald Sanders defines tact as "an intuitive perception of what is proper or fitting; the mental ability of saying and doing the right thing at the right time, so as not to unnecessarily offend or anger. This qualification is sadly often conspicuous by its absence, and the worker spoils the very work about which he is so concerned." (*The Divine Art of Soul-Winning,* Moody Press, pp. 31-32).

Acts 16 tells the conversion experience of two people. One of them, Lydia, listened quietly and then in a matter-of-fact way opened her life to Christ; whereas the other, the jailer, experienced a sudden, dramatic, emotional conversion.

Some people come to Christ gently and others come with a skip and a jump. The important thing is that they come. God is sovereign and does not deal with all people in exactly the same way. Jesus healed at least three blind men during His earthly ministry and used a different approach each time.

On a few occasions, Jesus even used the shock approach. After listening to a choice compliment from Nicodemus, He bluntly answered, "I tell you the truth, unless a man is born again, he cannot see the kingdom of God" (John 3:2-3). Such an approach must always be used with great insight. Though Jesus was direct at times, He was always caring.

There is a saying, "If you want to gather honey, don't kick over the beehive." We need to be sensitive in every area, especially in our conversation. Avoid critical comments about other churches. You may be sold on your church, but be sensitive and self-effacing. Seek to lift up Jesus and to honor the Scriptures.

Remember to be warm and caring, even if your witness is

refused. Our responsibility is to share the Good News adequately and lovingly. If we do that, we have fulfilled our responsibility. Though we all enjoy reaping, we must remember that Jesus Christ is Lord of the harvest, and He gives the increase.

Peter challenges, "Above all, love each other deeply, because love covers over a multitude of sins" (1 Peter 4:8). Love also covers a multitude of mistakes!

I have found that if my love is right, likely I will not be offensive. The Apostle Paul also reminds us that apart from God's love "we are nothing" (see 1 Cor. 13:2).

Relax. It seems to me that fear, more than anything else, hinders witnessing. By nature, I have a shy streak. It was especially difficult for me to be at ease witnessing until I began to claim God's strength and recognize my position in Christ. To begin with, I read and memorized such verses as Romans 8:31, "If God is for us, who can be against us?" Always remember that the all-powerful, all-knowing God is for you. At times you may be down on yourself, but God is enthusiastically for you. That is a life-changing truth, so lay hold of it, and you will receive strength to begin.

Often I have repeated and claimed 1 Corinthians 15:57, "But thanks be to God! He gives us the victory through our Lord Jesus Christ." Victory is promised to each of us through Jesus Christ—victory over fear, shyness, lack of ability, and even lack of training.

In our day, a popular philosophy abounds based on the innate goodness and resourcefulness of man. Peddlers of hope urge everyone to help himself to success, power, and happiness. But that concept is unbiblical. The message of Scripture is not to help yourself, but rather to *yield yourself* (see John 15:5). As you yield, you can experience God's strength to witness.

In and of myself I can't witness faithfully, but through Christ, I can. Philippians 4:13 reads, "I can do everything through Him who gives me strength." A key to conquering fear and timidity is realizing that Jesus Christ is our strength. I can't, but God can. When I look within, I become discouraged. I see my faults and shortcomings, but in Christ all the obstacles are cut down to their true size. Christ is able! When I look at our world, I'm overwhelmed by what I see, but when I look to Christ, I can rise above the obstacles. For every need any Christian has, there is a corresponding supply in Jesus Christ.

For many years, I carried a small card in my wallet with the words of 1 John 4:4 printed on it. Often I took it out and reminded myself, "The One who is in you is greater than the one who is in the world." That verse alone greatly increased my courage.

PHYSICAL PREPARATION

I have a pastor friend who is gifted in many ways. For example, he is a spiritual person with a good mind. He excels in the important areas of teaching. However, he has always been careless in his personal appearance. He pastors a rather affluent church in a mid-size college town. Some of his people are less than ecstatic about his wardrobe and general grooming. He lamented the situation and then in a matter of fact way asked, "What would you do if you were in my shoes?" Laughingly, I replied, "I'd shine them." From there, I lovingly shared about the importance of careful physical preparation. 1 Samuel 16:7 applies here, "Do not consider his appearance or his height, for I have rejected him. The Lord does not look at the things man looks at. *Man looks at the outward appearance,* but the Lord looks at the heart" (italics mine).

God is primarily interested in the heart. He sees the real me. If the heart is not right, nothing will be right.

But always remember that the people we share with see only the outward appearance, and their evaluation is based for the most part on external appearance. Therefore, when we witness, we will want to be sensitive regarding our outward appearance.

Good grooming and attractiveness are assets to witnessing. A man wearing unshined shoes and baggy pants can hinder his witness. Extreme color combinations, or immodest clothing can hurt our attempts to share the Good News. It is helpful to dress in such a way as to support our witness rather than undermine it. Balance is the key. Women should dress attractively and modestly. Neatness helps establish confidence and acceptance. Guard against anything that's offensive. Ask a quality friend to examine you regarding physical preparation.

It might be helpful to recall the elaborate preparation involved by an obstetrician about to deliver a baby. Each step is cared for meticulously. Surely we will not want to do less regarding a spiritual birth.

REMINDERS
● Clean hands and a pure heart are indispensable assets to witnessing.
● God loves people and so must we.
● Before we speak to people about God, it is important that we speak to God about people.
● The message of Scripture is not "help yourself," but rather "yield yourself."
● "If you want to gather honey, don't kick over the beehive."

The best argument for Christianity is Christians — their joy, their certainty, their completeness. But when the strongest argument against Christianity is also Christians; when they are somber and joyless, when they are self-righteous and smug, then Christianity dies a thousand deaths.

Sheldon Vanauken (*A Severe Mercy*, Harper & Row, p. 85)

If God is the evangelist and we are his instruments, perfection is not required to witness. God even used Balaam's ass to convey a message when he had to. If we desire to please the Lord and try to live a consistent life, we must *not* allow the enemy to seal our lips by overwhelming us with an awareness of our failures. We do not invite people to become Christians because we are perfect, but because Jesus Christ is perfect.

Paul Little (*Guide to Evangelism*, InterVarsity Press, p. 14).

EIGHT
Presenting Our Witness

No one calls for a doctor until he's sick. In the same way, until people understand the reality of sin and its results, they will probably show little interest in God's remedy.

Before we consider *how to present* a witness, a few reminders are in order. How we communicate the Good News is nearly as important as what we communicate. Our attitude and approach communicates as well as what we say. If we share expecting to find a warm, vital interest, we are more likely to receive a good reception. Enthusiasm is contagious. Try to enjoy the responses and questions of those with whom you share, even if at times you cannot answer all their questions. Often, I admit my inability and promise to find the answers.

In sharing our faith we need to be as natural as we can possibly be. Remember, our primary responsibility is to *sow the seed.* It is the work of the Holy Spirit to convict and convert. Though we're concerned, there's no need to be uptight. Often a casual comment will do more to create openness than anything else we might say.

Often I begin with a simple question like, "Are you interested in spiritual things?" or possibly, "What do you think about Jesus?" Regardless of the answer given, these questions open the way to share the Gospel. The important thing in all our witnessing is to be thoughtful of the rights of others and sensitive to the guidance of the Holy Spirit.

In presenting the Gospel I try to casually include several areas.

SHOW PEOPLE THEIR NEED OF SALVATION

The Bible teaches that every person has a spiritual need. If it is appropriate, I like to open my Bible and read directly from the Scriptures. At times, this is neither possible nor appropriate. I am reminded of the comment of Robert Murray McCheyne: "It is not our comment on the Word that saves, but the Word itself." If the occasion feels right, I might ask the one to whom I'm witnessing to read the verse. For example, Romans 3:23 states, "For all have sinned and fall short of the glory of God."

After reading that verse, I explain that some people have obviously sinned much less than others, but the fact is we have all sinned. All have come short of what God requires. We have failed in thought and word, as well as deed. Each one of us has a deep spiritual need, and none of us can meet that need by his own efforts.

At times I turn to the Old Testament and refer to Isaiah 53:6, "We all, like sheep, have gone astray, each of us has turned to his own way; and the Lord has laid on Him the iniquity of us all."

The first part of that verse, "We all, like sheep, have gone astray," states clearly the human condition. The second part of the verse, "the Lord has laid on Him the iniquity of us all," tells of God's provision of Christ as our sacrificial lamb.

Occasionally, I follow the reading of this verse with a number of questions. For example, "Bill, have you neglected spiritual matters? Have you pursued your own agenda of life to the neglect of God's will? Do you sense a void in your life? If so, according to this verse and other verses, you need to turn to Christ and allow Him to redirect your life."

SHOW PEOPLE THEY CANNOT SAVE THEMSELVES

Probably the greatest error that exists today is the belief that salvation is the result of our human effort; that is, that we can gain salvation by doing good things. I like to turn to the passages which tell us plainly that no one can save himself, such as:

"He saved us, not because of righteous things we had done, but because of His mercy" (Titus 3:5).

"Know that a man is not justified by observing the law, because by observing the law no one will be justified" (Gal. 2:16).

"For whoever keeps the whole law and yet stumbles at just one point is guilty of breaking all of it" (James 2:10).

"There is a way that seems right to a man, but in the end it leads to death" (Prov. 14:12).

Thousands imagine themselves Christian because they attempt to live by the Golden Rule or because they live decent, moral lives. Others rely upon their religious activity or even church membership. In direct contrast, the Apostle John states that salvation does not come through "the will of the flesh" (John 1:13, KJV).

The Bible message is plain on the subject and easy to understand. "For it is by grace you have been saved, through faith — and this not from yourselves, it is the gift of God — not by works, so that no one can boast" (Eph. 2:8-9).

Salvation is not something you do, but *Someone* you receive. Salvation is Jesus Christ. It would be easier to tunnel through a mountain with teaspoons than to get to heaven by one's personal effort, character, or morality. Salvation is *an offer,* not a demand. It is *not* based on what I do but what *Jesus Christ has done.*

We cannot become Christians by climbing the ladder of good works, rung by rung. Rather, Jesus Christ came down the ladder by way of Bethlehem's manger and Calvary's cross to meet us where we were. No one can ever save himself.

SHOW GOD'S PROVISION FOR SALVATION
The Good News is that God intervened in history to provide salvation for people like you and me. Paul announces it in Romans 5:8, "But God demonstrates His own love for us in this: While we were yet sinners, Christ died for us."

God's provision for our sin is seen in the best known verse in the Bible, "For God so loved the world that He gave His one and only Son, that whoever believes in Him shall not perish but have eternal life" (John 3:16). Years ago I discovered the importance of asking simple questions. After reading John 3:16 I like to ask, "Who is God's Son? What did Jesus do for you on the cross? What does 'whoever' mean? If you believe in God's Son according to this verse, what will you receive?" All the conversation is directed toward presenting Jesus as God's provision for man's sin. Jesus emphatically stated, "I am the way and the truth and the life. No one comes to the Father except through Me" (John 14:6).

I try to emphasize the importance of genuine repentance and faith.

What is repentance? It is turning away from whatever is displeasing to God. It is to turn from our way to God's way. It involves a change of heart, attitude, and mind.

What is faith? It is believing. It is receiving. It is not mere mental assent to a fact; rather it is a trust in a Person. It is relying on Jesus Christ *alone* for salvation and forgiveness for sin.

Often I like to ask the person to read John 3:36, pointing out the importance of trusting Christ, "Whoever believes in the Son has eternal life, but whoever rejects the Son will not see life, for God's wrath remains on him." At this point I usually ask, "Would you like to receive Jesus Christ as your personal Savior?"

Then I like to pray a simple prayer of preparation, "Heavenly Father, may this be the moment of salvation for Bill. To the best of his ability, may he repent of his sins and wholly place his faith in Jesus Christ who died for him."

While our heads are bowed in prayer, I often suggest that the person to whom I'm witnessing pray the following prayer out loud after me, phrase by phrase:

Lord Jesus, I invite You into my life right now. I confess that I am a sinner. I have been trusting in myself and my own efforts. But now I place my full trust in Jesus Christ alone. I believe You died on the cross for me. I accept You right now as my Savior and Lord. Help me to turn from my sins and follow You. Thank You for receiving me into Your eternal family. Amen.

SHOW HOW TO HAVE ASSURANCE OF SALVATION

The Apostle Paul encourages believers to "examine yourselves to see whether you are in the faith" (2 Cor. 13:5). Peter admonishes, "Be all the more eager to make your calling and election sure" (2 Peter 1:10). In other words, assurance is possible and even expected. The assurance of salvation is one of God's beautiful gifts to each believer. How can we know we are accepted by God?

We can know by the Word of God. We begin with the Bible. Assurance of salvation is based on acceptance of the Bible as Word of God. As we apply the promises of Scripture to our lives, doubt is resolved.

The Apostle John knew the difficulties of doubt. John wrote,

"I write these things to you who believe in the name of the Son of God so that you may know that you have eternal life" (1 John 5:13). That verse should be memorized. The purpose is that "you may *know* that you have eternal life." The word *know* means "to recognize the quality of." The Apostle John wrote these verses so that each believer might consciously recognize his position in Christ. This is not an opinion or a matter of inference but a revelation from God.

We can know by the witness within. Assurance of salvation is possible by the inner witness of the Holy Spirit. At conversion the believer becomes the dwelling place of the Holy Spirit. Yielding to the indwelling Holy Spirit brings a definite sense of assurance of salvation.

Some believers, through carelessness or lack of knowledge, grieve the Holy Spirit and know little or nothing of the witness of the Holy Spirit within. Paul said, "You received the Spirit of sonship. And by Him we cry, 'Abba, Father' " (Rom. 8:15), or literally, "My own dear Father." The Holy Spirit, who dwells in believers, witnesses to our spirits that we *are* God's children.

SHOW THAT JESUS WILL ENABLE BELIEVERS TO OVERCOME TEMPTATION

God's Word declares, "Therefore, if anyone is in Christ, he is a new creation; the old has gone, the new has come!" (2 Cor. 5:17). And the Word assures, "No temptation has seized you except what is common to man. And God is faithful; He will not let you be tempted beyond what you can bear. But when you are tempted, He will also provide a way out so that you can stand up under it" (1 Cor. 10:13).

How can we overcome temptation?

First, to the believer is given the privilege of prayer in confronting and overcoming temptation. James says, "If any of you lacks wisdom, he should ask God, who gives generously" (James 1:5).

Do you need help in overcoming your weakness? *Ask God!* Do you need deliverance from the power and temptation of sin? *Ask God!* He is able to deliver you. Often I have cried out, "Lord, help me," and God's deliverance was given. D.L. Moody said, "When Christians find themselves exposed to temptation, they should pray to God to uphold them, and when they are tempted they should not be discouraged. It is not a sin to be tempted; the sin is to yield to temptation."

Second, apply the Word of God. Jesus put Satan to flight by quoting Scripture, and we must defend ourselves the same way.

Third, submit to the indwelling Holy Spirit. To the believer who is led by the Holy Spirit, temptation will come, but it will not be able to destroy him. Because God has promised, "The One who is in you is greater than the one who is in the world" (1 John 4:4).

In your hour of trial, remember that God *is faithful.* He knows your capacity. He will give you all the strength you need to overcome temptation, or He will make a way of escape for you.

ADDITIONAL HELPS

Some organizations have prepared booklets and tracts to aid you in presenting the Good News. For over a century the Moody Bible Institute has published the little booklet, "Four Things God Wants You to Know." It contains appropriate Scripture verses about the way of salvation. Millions of copies have been effectively used around the world.

There is also the popular "Four Spiritual Laws" produced by Campus Crusade for Christ that many have used with great success.

I encourage you to start where you are, with what you know, and lovingly present the Good News.

REMINDERS

● The Good News is that God interevened in history to provide salvation for sinful people like you and me.

● Yielding to the indwelling Holy Spirit brings definite assurance of salvation.

● Salvation is an offer, not a demand.

● Jesus put Satan to flight by quoting Scripture, and we also must fortify ourselves with the Word of God.

● "When Christians find themselves exposed to temptation, they should pray to God to uphold them, and when they are tempted, they should not be discouraged. It is not a sin to be tempted; the sin is to fall into temptation" (D.L. Moody).

HOW TO PRESENT THE GOSPEL

1. Show people their need of salvation (Rom. 3:23; Rom. 6:23; Isa. 53:6).

2. Show them they cannot save themselves (Titus 3:5; Gal. 2:16; Prov. 14:12).

3. Show them God's provision for their salvation (Rom. 5:8; John 3:16; John 14:6; John 1:12).

4. Show them how to have the assurance of salvation (1 John 5:13; Rom. 10:9; 1 John 1:9).

5. Show them that Jesus Christ will enable believers to overcome temptation (2 Cor. 5:17; 1 Cor. 10:13).

VERSES TO COMMIT TO MEMORY

"For all have sinned and fall short of the glory of God" (Rom. 3:23).

"For the wages of sin is death, but the gift of God is eternal life in Christ Jesus our Lord" (Rom. 6:23).

"We all, like sheep, have gone astray, each of us has turned to his own way; and the Lord has laid on Him [Christ] the iniquity of us all" (Isa. 53:6).

"He saved us, not because of righteous things we had done, but because of His mercy. He saved us through the washing of rebirth and renewal by the Holy Spirit" (Titus 3:5).

"There is a way that seems right to a man, but in the end it leads to death" (Prov. 14:12).

"For it is by grace you have been saved, through faith—and this not from yourselves, it is the gift of God—not by works, so that no one can boast" (Eph. 2:8-9).

"But God demonstrates His own love for us in this: While we were still sinners, Christ died for us" (Rom. 5:8).

"For God so loved the world that He gave His one and only Son, that whoever believes in Him shall not perish but have eternal life" (John 3:16).

"To all who received Him [Christ], to those who believed in His name, He gave the right to become children of God" (John 1:12).

"I write these things to you who believe in the name of the Son of God so that you may know that you have eternal life" (1 John 5:13).

"Therefore, if anyone is in Christ, he is a new creation; the old has gone, the new has come!" (2 Cor. 5:17).

"Jesus answered, 'I am the way and the truth and the life. No one comes to the Father except through me' " (John 14:6).

"That if you confess with your mouth, 'Jesus is Lord,' and believe in your heart that God raised Him from the dead, you will be saved. For it is with your heart that you believe and are justified, and it is with your mouth that you confess and are saved" (Rom. 10:9-10).

"If we confess our sins, He is faithful and just and will forgive us our sins and purify us from all unrighteousness" (1 John 1:9).

"Know that a man is not justified by observing the law, but by faith in Jesus Christ. So we, too, have put our faith in Christ Jesus that we may be justified by faith in Christ and not by observing the law, because by observing the law no one will be justified" (Gal. 2:16).

People often ask, "If Christianity is true, why do the majority of intelligent people not believe it?" The answer is precisely the same as the reason the majority of unintelligent people don't believe it. They don't want to because they're unwilling to accept the moral demands it would make on their lives. . . . There isn't a thing you or I can do with a man who, despite all evidence to the contrary, insists that black is white.

We ourselves must be convinced about the truth we proclaim. Otherwise we won't be at all convincing to other people. We must be able to say confidently with Peter, "We did not follow cleverly devised myths when we made known to you the power and coming of our Lord Jesus Christ" (2 Peter 1:16). Then our witness will ring with authority, conviction, and the power of the Holy Spirit.

> Paul E. Little, (*How to Give Away Your*
> *Faith,* InterVarsity Press, pp. 131–132)

Novelist Ayn Rand had mesmerized a student audience at Yale University with her prickly ideas. Afterward a reporter from *Time* magazine asked her, "Miss Rand, what's wrong with the modern world?"

Without hesitation she replied, "Never before has the world been so desperately asking for answers to crucial questions, and never before has the world been so frantically committed to the idea that no answers are possible.

"To paraphrase the Bible," she continued, "the modern attitude is, 'Father, forgive us, for we know not what we are doing—and please don't tell us!' "

It is to such a generation that God has called today's Christians to minister—in an age which sees everything that was nailed down coming loose, a time when things happen which people once thought could never happen.

> Howard G. Hendricks (*Say It with Love,*
> Victor Books, p. 23)

NINE
Popular Questions and Objections

T o witness faithfully we need to know *why* we believe as well as *what* we believe. Each Christian will want to learn to defend his faith. The Bible instructs us to "always be prepared to give an answer to everyone who asks you to give the reason for the hope that you have. But do this with gentleness and respect" (1 Peter 3:15).

To effectively share the Gospel, we must be convinced of its authority in our own lives. Witnessing cannot be sustained for very long unless the mind and heart agree. Also, we have the privilege and responsibility *to give answers* to those who have sincere questions.

I am not suggesting for a minute that we know all the answers. We don't! However, there are answers to many of the common questions that may be asked.

"I DON'T BELIEVE THE BIBLE."
Often, as I have shared my faith, the person will respond, "I don't believe the Bible." Usually it is best to take that very objection as your starting point for a presentation of the Good

News. Remember, however, that Peter and Paul taught the Scriptures, even though their hearers made *no* pretense of believing the Bible, whereupon the Holy Spirit took the Scriptures and applied them in such a way that many believed. Although we want to defend the faith wisely, we should always remember that witnessing is primarily a proclamation of the faith.

When people say that the Bible is full of errors, often they are hiding behind a false objection. Usually I ask what particular Scripture is troubling them. If I know the answer, I share it. If I do not, I tell them, "I don't know the answer, but I'll find the answer."

If the person objecting has read little of the Bible, you will quickly be able to tell that the objection is insincere. However, under no circumstances, should we ever treat lightly a person's objections. Some passages of Scripture are difficult to answer. A knowledge of the surrounding verses often provides the answer.

Two persuasive arguments are the transforming power of the Bible and the reliability of Scripture over the centuries. (Further help is available in the book *Evidence That Demands a Verdict*, by Josh McDowell, Here's Life Publishers.)

"IS JESUS CHRIST THE ONLY WAY TO GOD?"
Some people believe that as long as an individual is *sincere*, God will be satisfied. In other words, the earnest Hindu or Muslim will be accepted because he too worships God, although under a different name.

But the issue is not how we view various religions, but *what is truth*. Sincerity is commendable, but it is not the deciding factor. For example, some religions recognize Jesus as a great teacher but not as the Son of God. They deny His deity, His atoning death, and His literal resurrection. Yet Jesus plainly said in John 14:6, "I am the way, and the truth, and the life, no one comes to the Father, except through Me." According to Jesus Himself, there is no other way to God, and that is where the Christian stands. It is not a matter of stubbornness but rather our responsibility to present truth as revealed in the Bible.

"WHAT ABOUT THE HEATHEN?"

There are some people who reject the Gospel because they cannot believe that a righteous God will judge people who have never heard the Good News. This is not an easy objection to answer. In attempting to answer this, three things must be kept in mind.

First, the Scriptures teach that *God is just.* We can have complete confidence that whatever He does with those who have not heard the Gospel will be right. God must be trusted.

Second, God has spoken throughout history in many ways. One of those ways is through His creation. Why? "Since what may be known about God is plain to them, because God has made it plain to them. For since the creation of the world God's invisible qualities — His eternal power and divine nature — have been clearly seen, being understood from what has been made, so that men are without excuse" (Rom. 1:19-20).

God has spoken to everyone through *creation* and also through *human conscience.* To neglect or reject God in the light of His creation and His voice to human consciousness is to leave people without excuse.

Third, the final judgment will be based upon what each individual has done with Jesus. The issue will not be the fate of the heathen, but rather what have I personally done with Jesus Christ? The Scriptures tell us that "no one comes to the Father, except through Christ" (John 14:6; see Acts 4:12). That places significant responsibility upon each believer to bring the message to the unreached of our world.

"WOULD A GOD OF LOVE JUDGE MEN AND WOMEN?"

Another objection for rejecting the Gospel is the one given by people who will not believe that a God of love could condemn anyone. God *is* love, that is true, but He is also just and righteous. As such, He cannot allow sin or a sinful person to violate His standards in His presence. The prophet Habakkuk wrote, "Your eyes are too pure to look on evil; You cannot tolerate wrong" (1:13). God loves each person, but when men and women willfully neglect and reject God's love, they are the ones who separate themselves from God in the present and for eternity.

"I'M AFRAID I CAN'T LIVE THE CHRISTIAN LIFE."
Some people are afraid to accept the Gospel because they're afraid of failing. No one can live the Christian life in his own strength. It's impossible. But when a person receives Jesus Christ, the Holy Spirit of God indwells him (Eph. 1:13; Rom. 8:9). It is the Holy Spirit who keeps us going and gives us divine strength to go on with God. Without the enabling power of God and the indwelling Holy Spirit, failure is inevitable.

"WHAT ABOUT THE MIRACLES OF THE BIBLE?"
Another objection that people give for their delay is that they cannot believe some of the miracles of the Bible. My answer to the question of Bible miracles is found in the three-letter word *God.* If God is God, He has the ability to do anything. He is all-powerful. The Bible has proved itself trustworthy in the past, and there is good reason for trusting it in the present. God can and does intervene in the world that He has created.

"HOW DO YOU ACCOUNT FOR HUMAN SUFFERING?"
The Bible speaks of the suffering of Job. In the depth of his experience he cried, "Why did I not perish at birth, and die as I came from the womb?" (3:11). Job suffered the loss of wealth, family, and health. Each of us at times have asked, "Why? Why are some born blind and others disabled? Why do we have wars? If God is all-powerful, why does He allow evil?"

I do not believe anyone can fully answer those questions, and we ought to say so. However, let me suggest some areas to consider.

The Scriptures teach that God created a perfect world which was marred by the entrance of sin (see Gen. 3:14-15). All suffering is directly or indirectly related to the Fall of man. Because man violated God's law, evil exists in this world.

Added to that is the fact that we are individuals, with the power to choose. We can choose good or evil. We're not robots. Often suffering is the result of our own rebellious wills (see Gen. 1:26-27; 3:6-13). Within God's rule we can choose and reap the fruits of our choices. David chose Bathsheba and immorality and reaped the consequences. Much of the suffering in this world is the result of our own choices.

Then too there are times when suffering appears to be for the greater glory of God, as illustrated in John 9:1-3. Believers in Christ often claim the promise of Romans 8:28, "And we know that in all things God works for the good of those who love Him, who have been called according to His purpose." Suffering at times may not appear to benefit me for the present moment, yet I can rest in the knowledge that the experience is for my ultimate good. It is foolish to speculate about the origin of evil. Rather, we should recognize the fact of evil and recognize that the only solution is found in Jesus Christ.

"WON'T GOD FORGIVE ME IF I LIVE A MORAL LIFE?"
For God to forgive sin without dealing with it would be contrary to His nature and righteous rule. God is holy. "Justice and judgment are the habitation of Thy throne" (Ps. 89:14, KJV).

Also, the Bible teaches, "All our righteous acts are like filthy rags" (Isa. 64:6). "So those controlled by the sinful nature cannot please God" (Rom. 8:8). The Bible teaches that even the best moral life falls short of what God requires (Rom. 3:23). No morality or work of ours could ever merit God's forgiveness or make us acceptable. Sin *must be dealt with* and removed. That is only possible through the atoning death of Jesus Christ.

At times I have been unable to give what might be called a satisfying answer. Yet substantial progress was made by being a *concerned listener* and showing *genuine interest*. Always remember that agnostics and atheists face greater unanswered questions in their unbelief.

A graduate from the University of Moscow and life-long Communist committed himself to Christ. When I asked him what convinced him more than anything else to become a Christian, he answered, "The love and interest of other Christians."

May we "be ready always to give an answer" (1 Peter 3:15), but also remember that "faith comes from hearing the message, and the message is heard through the word of Christ" (Rom. 10:17).

For further information on objections, see *Know Why You Believe*, by Paul Little (Victor Books) and *Objections Answered* by R.C. Sproul (Ligonier Valley Study Center).

SOME THINGS FOR THE WITNESS TO REMEMBER

As the witness presses this battle to the heart of the lost person in soulful compassion, let him remember the following principles as outlined by L.R. Scarborough in his book *A Search for Souls* (Sunday School Board of the Southern Baptist Convention, pp. 125-26):

1. *Christ and His Spirit are with him, even by his side and within his very heart.* The Holy Spirit aids, He loves, He longs, He intercedes for him and for the sinner. He presses with him and through him His message. You are not alone. He says, "I am with you when you go to make disciples and teach them."

2. *Remember His word is powerful, sharper than any two-edged sword.* His Gospel is the power of God unto salvation and it will not return void. It will accomplish that for which He sent it.

3. *Remember that no case is too hard for Christ and His Gospel.*

"He is able to save completely those who come to God through Him" (Heb. 7:25). Have faith in Christ and His truth.

4. *Remember that it is Christ and His Gospel that save.* You cannot save the soul of anyone; sentiment and tear-stories won't save. Christ will. Do not deceive the sinner. Do not give him a stone for bread. He needs Christ, only Christ, all of Christ, and Christ offers Himself through you.

5. *Remember that "faint heart never won fair lady."* Be bold, be brave, be persistent. Do not give up easily. Your adversary the devil never gives up. George Muller kept on sixty-two years after one man and won him. I know a wife who prayed every day for forty years for her husband and won him. God says we shall reap if we faint not.

6. *Remember the prize is worth the noblest effort.* You deal with immortal souls, dear to God, to Christ, and to you. If I were to live a thousand years and win one soul to Christ, my life would have been immeasurably worthwhile if I did nothing else; but I should win souls every day, whether I live long or short. If I had ten thousand lives, I would give every one of them full-length for winning souls and serving Christ.

Whence comes the patience that is so indispensable for evangelistic work? From dwelling on the fact that God is sovereign in grace and that His Word does not return void; that it is He who gives us such opportunities as we find for sharing our knowledge of Christ with others, and that He is able in His own good time to enlighten them and bring them to faith.

> J.I. Packer (*Evangelism and the Sovereignty of God,* InterVarsity Press, p. 121)

TEN
Seeking Commitments

From Genesis through the Book of Revelation, the hand of God reaches out to welcome us. The Book of Genesis pictures God calling to Noah, "Come thou and all thy house into the ark" (Gen. 7:1, KJV). The word *come* is used more than 600 times in the Bible. God is so interested in our union that through direct invitation, by parables, types, and symbols, He continually invites us to come to Him. The Bible closes with a loving, urgent, all-inclusive appeal, "The Spirit and the bride say, 'Come!' And let him who hears say, 'Come!' Whoever is thirsty, let him come; and whoever wishes, let him take the free gift of the water of life" (Rev. 22:17).

When we witness we have the opportunity to share God's invitation and seek a commitment. It is not only our responsibility to share what God has done through Jesus Christ; we must also tell what God *expects men and women to do.*

WHY SHOULD WE SEEK A DECISION?

We have the constant example of Scripture. As we review the ministry of God's servants in the Bible, we discover a common characteristic in their dealings with people. Consider just a few illustrations.

While Moses was receiving the Law, the Children of Israel became restless and rebellious. Their dissatisfaction resulted in carelessness and idolatry. They ate, drank, and corrupted themselves in idolatrous worship (Ex. 32:6-8). When Moses returned and saw their idolatry, he became angry. He burned the golden calf that they were worshiping, ground it to powder, and threw the ashes upon the waters. The next day Moses called the people together and urged them to make a decision. "So he stood at the entrance to the camp and said, 'Whoever is for the Lord, come to me' " (32:26). And many came and stood by Moses.

Joshua, the successor of Moses, also sought a commitment. At Shechem he challenged the people, "Choose for yourselves this day whom you will serve" (Josh. 24:15). And the people responded. It is interesting to notice that Joshua recorded the decision of the people in the Book of the Law of God and then erected a *"decision card" of stone* as witness to their response (vv. 26-27).

King Josiah likewise called upon the Children of Israel to renew their vows to the Lord. He himself "renewed the covenant in the presence of the Lord—to follow the Lord and keep His commands, regulations and decrees with all his heart and all his soul, and to obey the words of the covenant written in this book" (2 Chron. 34:31).

Josiah went a step further. The next verse reads, "Then he had everyone . . . pledge themselves to it" (2 Chron. 34:32). Josiah felt that his witness was incomplete until there was a visible affirmation of purpose. Josiah sought a decision. Ezra and Nehemiah did the same. The Scriptures abound with examples of God's servants seeking a verdict.

Jesus also set an example for us. He came saying, "Repent and believe the Good News!" (Mark 1:15). To Peter and Andrew

He called, "*Come, follow me,* and I will make you fishers of men" (Mark 1:17). Jesus continually pressed for a decision.

Howard Hendricks has written, "The entire New Testament is a record of the continuing entreaty of the Lord toward a world He had already died to redeem. God didn't just *say,* 'Be saved'; He said it with the highest degree of love" (*Say It with Love,* Victor Books, p. 15).

Staggering though it may seem, God is calling people through you and me today. Charles B. Williams translates 2 Corinthians 5:20, "So I am an envoy to represent Christ, because it is through me that God is making His appeal. As one representing Christ I beg you, be reconciled to God." We must realize that the Almighty God is calling men and women through what we are, say, and do.

Someone might ask, "Is it right to attempt to persuade a person to receive Jesus Christ?" I believe it is. But we should remember that although Jesus sought sinners, He never forced anyone to come to Him. In Mark 10:21 we are told that Jesus, inviting the rich young ruler to follow Him, "loved him." Yet, when this man turned away, Jesus did not run after him. Jesus did not stiff-arm His way into his life. Our Lord spoke with him and loved him, but He did not force him to respond.

The Apostle Paul used all his God-given wisdom and logic to bring those to whom he witnessed to the place of decision. On one occasion Paul wrote, "Since, then, we know what it is to fear the Lord, we try to persuade men" (2 Cor. 5:11). A study of the Book of Acts presents Paul as a serious persuader.

WHY DO SOME HESITATE TO SEEK A DECISION?

Here are several possible reasons some people hesitate to seek a commitment.

Misunderstanding. Some people feel there is a logical inconsistency between God's sovereignty and human responsibility. Many of us at sometime or other have wrestled with the problem. At times it is extremely difficult to know where the Spirit stops and the flesh begins. It is indeed a serious and sensitive area.

J. I. Packer writes in *Evangelism and the Sovereignty of God* (InterVarsity Press):

> What the Bible does is to assert both truths side by side in the strongest and most unambiguous terms as two ultimate facts; this, therefore, is the position that we must take in our own thinking. C.H. Spurgeon was once asked if he could reconcile these two truths to each other. 'I wouldn't try,' he replied; 'I never reconcile friends.' Friends? — yes, *friends.* This is the point that we have to grasp. In the Bible, divine sovereignty and human responsibility are not enemies. They are not uneasy neighbors; they are not in an endless state of cold war with each other. They are *friends*, and they work together.

Occasionally, someone will suggest that since the unconverted are dead spiritually and dead people can't respond, believers should not try to persuade them. But is it true that we should not ask people to do what they cannot do? Jesus called Lazarus, who was dead, and a dead man did what he could not do: Lazarus came forth (John 11:44). Jesus told the impotent man, "Get up! Pick up your mat and walk," and he did (John 5:8). To the man with the withered hand, Jesus said, "Stretch out your hand," and he responded (Mark 3:5).

We need to remember that the God who calls men and women to come also gives them the ability to come. God calls people to make decisions through you and me. That is an awesome truth.

Fear. In witnessing, some might fail to seek a decision because of fear. Fear of failure is very real. But when we realize the message we have, the value of an individual soul, the blessedness of heaven, and the reality of hell, we dare not allow fear to keep us from seeking a commitment. As witnesses, we need to pray that the seed will fall upon responsive soil and then do what we can to encourage a decision.

Fatigue. It is possible to give all our thoughts and efforts in preparation and presentation and fail to prepare for the closing moments of appeal. When we consider the privilege we have, however, all other considerations must be laid aside. Philip the deacon (Acts 8) followed through until the Ethiopian was fully satisfied; he "went on his way rejoicing" (8:39). By all means, give your very best to the strategic moment of response to faith in the Lord Jesus Christ.

HOW SHOULD WE SEEK A DECISION?

There are several things to keep in mind as you seek to guide a person to a decision.

Seek a decision lovingly. "Love covers over a multitude of sins" (1 Peter 4:8). Love also covers a multitude of mistakes we make in witnessing. We will not be offensive if we are mastered by the love of Christ. Divine love is gentle and not offensive. Love is considerate and always courteous.

Seek a decision believingly. The element of faith is very important. The Bible says that "without faith it is impossible to please God" (Heb. 11:6). The combination of love and faith if powerful, and each witness should earnestly cultivate both of those gifts. The example of Jesus encourages us to seek decisions.

REMINDERS

● From Genesis to Revelation, the loving hand of God reaches out to seek and save men and women.

● It is interesting to observe that Joshua recorded the decision of the people in the Book of the Law of God and then erected a "decision card" of stone as a witness to their response (Josh. 24:26-27).

● It is not only our responsibility to share and declare what God has done through Jesus Christ; we must also tell what God expects of men and women.

● Although Jesus sought sinners, He never coerced anyone.

● In the Bible, divine sovereignty and human responsibility are not enemies. They are not uneasy neighbors; they are not in an endless state of cold war with each other. They are *friends*, and they work together.

● The overwhelming testimony of Scripture, as well as the example of Jesus, indicates that by all means we should seek a verdict.

Henry Ford, the father of "mass production," is reported to have made the statement: "You can have any color Ford you want as long as it's black." His mass-producing manufacturing process required that everything be made exactly alike. While it is the goal of Christian nurture that each Christian be "Christlike," we must keep in mind that Christian lives *are not mass produced*. It takes months instead of minutes to establish a lasting Christian life . . . months (sometimes years) of painstaking, "hot-house" nursery vigilance and care of the seeds sown and/or reaped by evangelism.

Dr. James Kennedy (*Evangelism Explosion*, Tyndale, pp. 146–147).

ELEVEN

Follow-Up

One of our serious areas of weakness in evangelism is the care of new believers. Great effort is put forth in witnessing and bringing friends to the place of decision, but often they're neglected once they have received Christ. It is important to make a record of each decision. Too often we drift into an attitude of carelessness and imagine that the new Christian will automatically grow into a mature believer. Consider these guidelines for follow-up.

PREPARE A DECISION CARD

I have found it helpful to formulate a paragraph on a card that states simply and clearly the decision that has been made.

The Bible teaches that when you place your faith in Jesus Christ, you are born again by the "Word of God" (1 Peter 1:23). A decision card could serve as a spiritual birth certificate. It is a reminder of one's commitment to Jesus Christ. The decision card might be worded like this:

Today, ___(date)___ , I asked Jesus Christ to be my

Savior. The best I know how, I have committed my life to Him for forgiveness of all my sins and for His will for my life in the future. To the best of my ability, in dependence upon the Lord, I shall seek to witness to others concerning Jesus Christ.

<u>   (signature)   </u>

Encourage the new believer to keep it in his wallet or purse as a lifelong reminder of his decision.

USE HELPFUL LITERATURE

Another helpful thing to do in following up new believers is to supply them with helpful literature. Out of a sense of wanting to do more for new believers, I wrote the following letter:

Dear friend,

    I am so happy for your decision to accept Christ as your Savior, Lord, and Master. The Bible says, "Except a man be born again, he cannot see the kingdom of God" (John 3:3, KJV). Because you have committed yourself to Christ, you have become a child of God, and He has become your Heavenly Father.

    As a newborn child is cared for in the physical world, so you must be helped and instructed in spiritual matters.

    First, you should read the Bible systematically. The Gospel of John is a good place for you to begin. What food is to the body, the Bible is to the soul. At a prescribed time in a quiet place, each day should start with the Bible. This is a must if you are to grow in the things of God. Remember, at least a chapter a day. "The Bible will keep you from sin, or sin will keep you from the Bible."

    Second, you must learn to pray. Prayer is the communion of the believer with God. We speak to God, but He also speaks to us. Prayer is not merely asking favors of God but rather waiting in quietness before Him. Pray for personal cleansing and victory over evil. Pray for yourself and pray for others.

Third, you are to use every opportunity to confess Christ before the world. In a cheerful way, immediately tell someone of your spiritual decision. Activity always strengthens. When God's people witness to others, they develop a big appetite for Bible study. The result of their speaking to others of their new life will provide daily up-to-date subjects for prayer. When a new convert begins to share his faith, everything comes into proper focus. If you make a great deal of Christ, He will make a great deal of you; but if you make but little of Christ, Christ will make but little of you.

Fourth, you should find a church home. If a mother permits her children to grow up in idleness, the result will be untaught children. Since the Christian's duty is evident in this matter, waiting only forms bad habits. The Bible says, "Let us not give up meeting together, as some are in the habit of doing" (Heb. 10:25). Your faithful church attendance will help you in spiritual growth, Christian education, missions, and social outreach.

If you follow these four Bible principles, Christian growth is guaranteed. Doubtless you will meet with temptations; but you need not yield or fall, for God has promised, "Greater is He that is in you, than he that is in the world" (1 John 4:4, KJV). If you fall, seek immediate forgiveness. "If we confess our sins, He is faithful and just to forgive us our sins, and to cleanse us from all unrighteousness" (1 John 1:9, KJV). Do not remain defeated; get up and go right on. Perhaps you are facing the battle of some habit: remember that Christ is ready to help you, and He has all power in heaven and earth.

In short, the secret of successful Christian living is to keep your eyes on Christ. The best of people will fail you at times, but Jesus Christ never fails.

Sincerely yours,

At times it is only possible to follow up a person with a letter, Gospel tract, or booklet. However, in most cases, we can follow up with substantial literature and books.

To help meet the needs of the new believer, I wrote *How to Begin the Christian Life,* published by Moody Press. Many good books to help the new Christian are available. Be sure the ones you select are sound yet simple enough for the new Christian to understand.

APPOINT A SPIRITUAL GUARDIAN

Although a person may receive Jesus Christ in a relatively short period of time, a lifetime is involved in becoming like Jesus Christ. The goal for each new believer is to be conformed to the image of Jesus Christ (Rom. 8:29).

Christians are not mass produced. Just as a baby requires painstaking care, plenty of love, and constant attention, so each new believer needs tender love and care. There must be that personal care in follow-up. To be effective, follow-up should be personal, persistent, and purposeful.

Letters and literature are helpful, but nothing compares with the loving care of another Christian. Follow-up is most effective when it is *personal.*

Follow-up should also be *persistent.* Although it can be abused, persistence usually conveys that there is a deep, abiding interest. A loving persistence so often makes a difference.

By "purposeful," I mean our follow-up should lead into the fellowship of a local church.

Here is a checklist for the guardian:

1. Pray for the one you've been assigned to each day.
2. Warmly welcome him into your fellowship or group.
3. Visit him in his home. Observe his interests. Be aware of his likes and dislikes. Learn his special talents.
4. Arrange to sit with him in church if wise and possible.
5. Seek to introduce him into some other church function.
6. Invite him into your home.
7. Provide guidance for him in the Christian life.
8. Carefully notice any indications of error and attempt to correct him lovingly.

INTRODUCE THE NEW BELIEVER TO THE CHURCH

There is nothing on earth that is more significant in the growth of each believer than the church. Although the church has many critics, it has no rival. Jesus Christ is the foundation of the church (Eph. 1:22-23) and He has guaranteed its future (Matt. 16:18).

Environment is so very important. A tulip bulb on the sidewalk will not grow. If the bulb is placed in the soil, it has a promising future. Each new believer needs the fellowship of a local church and the friendship of God's people. The local church is vital and is God's means of accomplishing His work here on earth.

Actually, the Greek word *ekklesia*, which is translated "church" in the New Testament, refers to either a local assembly of Christian believers or else to the universal body of Christ made up of all people everywhere who have received Jesus Christ as Savior. In 1 Corinthians 1:2 we read, "All those everywhere who call on the name of our Lord Jesus Christ—their Lord and ours." This refers to the mystical body of Christ, often called the Bride of Christ, or the Church universal.

However, this same verse begins, "Unto the church of

God which is at Corinth." This plainly refers to the local congregation of believers at Corinth.

The word *ekklesia* is made up of two separate words, the preposition *ek*, meaning "out of," and the verb *kaleo*, meaning "to call." The Church is a called-out group of people, a people separated by God unto Himself. (Moody Press, pp. 128-29).

When the word *ekklesia* or church is found in the New Testament, it generally refers to a body of believers organized in a local community, accepting the Scriptures as the basis of faith and conduct.

As soon as possible, the new believer should be introduced to the opportunities and responsibilities of the local church. It could be through an orientation class, the Sunday School, or even an informal Bible study group from the church.

The task of the church is more than evangelization. It includes worship, encouragement, edification, training, fellowship, and world outreach. The Great Commission stresses "teaching them to obey everything I have commanded you" (Matt. 28:20). We must not only reach but teach and enlist.

New military recruits are enlisted and trained for the conflict. So we too must instruct each new believer to be ready for the conflicts of life. Through neglect, many new Christians never become fruitful even though their souls have been won.

REMINDERS
● So that the people would never forget, Joshua erected a "decision card" of stone as a memorial.
● A decision card is a kind of spiritual birth certificate.
● Christians are not mass produced. Just as a baby requires painstaking care, plenty of love, and loads of attention, so each believer needs tender love and care.
● Although the church has many critics, it has no rival.

And from Jesus Christ, who is the faithful witness, the first-born from the dead, and the ruler of the kings of the earth.

Revelation 1:5

Now it is *required* that those who have been given a trust must prove *faithful.*

1 Corinthians 4:2

Imagine that a sower is going down the line with his little pouch over his shoulder, and the pouch is filled with seed, and as he moves along down the line, he throws that seed with great dexterity. After all, he's been doing this all his life.

Let's also imagine he's got a five-year-old boy, and he's made him a little pouch to fit him. This little five-year-old guy is walking behind him with his fat, little, chubby hand and little short fingers. He sticks his little fist in his pouch, and he throws seed, and it goes every place. I mean, clumps of it land over here and piles of it hit his father in the back. And every once in a while he just throws a handful to the birds.

Do you want to know something? Whether the seed was thrown by the father, who is dexterous at it, or the fat little hand of his five-year-old son, if it hits good ground, what happens? Fruit.

John MacArthur (*The Kingdom Mission,*
1983 Founder's Week Messages, Moody
Bible Institute, p. 67)

TWELVE
Are We Responsible for Results?

F rancois Millet's famous painting, "The Sower," which hangs in the Boston Museum of Fine Art, captures the tension between the faithful sower "throwing seed" and fleeting time.

Each Christian is "a sower." The seed is "the good news of the Gospel," and Satan is our foe, but what about "the soil"? To witness faithfully, we need to understand the types of soil that receive the scattered seed.

Too often, in our witnessing the stress is placed upon results. However, more than we care to admit, all of us have experienced occasional indifference and even open hostility. A critical question to face is, Are *we* responsible for the results?

Let me hasten to say that we all enjoy the indescribable exhilaration of reaping a harvest, and that is how it should be; nevertheless, our primary goal is to faithfully sow the seed, regardless of outward results.

Several years ago I wrote a book titled *How to Witness Successfully*. I still cringe regarding the title because it fosters the error that the individual Christian is responsible for the success or failure in sowing the seed of the Gospel.

Matthew 13 teaches otherwise. This passage is commonly called "The Parable of the Sower." Upon careful review, however, it might better be titled "The Parable of the Soils." It is not primarily the talent, technique, or even the tears of the sower that bring results, as important as they may be; but, rather, the reception and response of the soil that determines the harvest. When a person gets hold of this truth, there is a release from false expectations. We must always remember that God alone gives the increase, as we faithfully sow the seed.

Though our primary concern in this chapter is to examine the kinds of soil, first consider "the sower" and "the seed."

Matthew 13:3 begins, "A farmer went out to sow his seed." Those listening to Jesus easily understood His language. Probably, Jesus pointed to a sower off in the distance scattering seed. However, it is important to remind ourselves that this parable is not primarily about the sower. In fact, the Scripture says nothing about the character of the sower or the method of sowing seed. This point was so crucial that Jesus said, "He who has ears, let him hear" (v. 9). Jesus really said, "Get this, because it is basic to faithful, long-haul sowing."

After we receive Jesus Christ, our natural inclination is to want to shout the Good News from the housetops, assuming that people will flock to receive Christ. The Gospel is such exciting news that we imagine people will respond in droves. But Jesus warns us and says, in effect, "Before you hurry off to witness, you need to understand that probably it's not going to be at all like that. You are to faithfully sow the seed, regardless of the result, and don't forget that there are different kinds of soil out there. This understanding is one of the secrets of a life of faithful witnessing."

But who is the sower? This particular parable does not answer that question. Therefore, it is reasonable to assume that the sower is anyone who sows the good seed of the Gospel. The sower could be the Lord, because we read in another parable toward the end of this same chapter, "The one who sowed the good seed is the Son of Man" (v. 37). However, in "The Parable of the Sower," the sower appears to be anyone who sows seed.

Briefly consider "the seed." What is the seed? Verse 19 says, "When anyone hears the message about the kingdom and does not understand it, the evil comes and snatches away what was sown in his heart. This is the seed sown along the path." The seed is "the message of the kingdom." The seed is "the Gospel"—the Good News of salvation. Luke 8:11 says "the seed is the Word of God." "The sower" is anyone who shares the Gospel, and "the seed" is the message of salvation by God's grace.

Consider the kinds of soil about which Jesus spoke.

THE WAYSIDE SOIL

"Some [seed] fell along the path, and the birds came and ate it up" (v. 4). No human being scatters seed perfectly. Some seed will fall upon the wayside path regardless of our skill or lack of skill. These paths were common, criss-crossing the entire countryside. Usually birds followed the sower, seeking especially the seed that fell on the path. What the birds didn't eat, the walking travelers trampled under foot.

The wayside hearer is described more fully in verse 19: "When anyone hears the message about the kingdom and does not understand it, the evil one comes and snatches away what was sown in his heart. This is the seed sown along the path." Apparently, these hear the Good News, but they are unresponsive and unreceptive. The seed does not take root. It lies on the surface exposed and unprotected. This individual is hardened and determined to exclude God from his life. There is nothing wrong with the sower. He is concerned, conscientious, and compassionate. There is nothing wrong with the seed. It is pure and good. The fundamental problem is the soil. It is hard, dry, insensitive, maybe even belligerent and unreceptive. It is of great importance to remember that at times the faithful witness will fall upon this kind of soil. When it does, don't be disheartened or defeated, but rather continue to sow the seed faithfully.

THE ROCKY SOIL

"Some fell on rocky places, where it did not have much soil" (v. 5). Israel is a land of rocks and mountains. In many places, there is a great amount of limestone under the soil, though often only inches from the surface. At times the farmer plows frightfully close to the rock. Some seed falls inevitably on the rocky ground where there is very little soil. Jesus comments about this type of person: "The one who received the seed that fell on rocky places is the man who hears the Word and at once receives it with joy. But since he has no root, he lasts only a short time. When trouble or persecution comes because of the Word, he quickly falls away" (vv. 20-21).

The rocky soil person is one who looks like the real thing, but there's no root. They glitter like a Fourth of July sparkler, but they burn out just as fast. Why? They never counted the cost. Verse 21 states "he has no root." Maybe they came because of the emotion of the moment. Possibly, they saw in the Good News a quick fix for a broken dream or a damaged relationship. Perhaps they were manipulated and massaged into some kind of external profession. At first they looked so good and sounded great. But what happened? When adversity appeared they quickly bailed out. Vance Havner used to say, "Some people go up like a rocket and come down like a rock." Why? The answer is no root. The Apostle John warns, "They went out from us, but they did not really belong to us" (1 John 2:19).

THE THORNY SOIL

"Other seed fell among thorns, which grew up and choked the plants' (v. 7). A more accurate translation of the word *thorn* is "weeds," and weeds grow better than anything else! This describes the person who hears the Gospel, but the daily cares of this life choke the seed, and he is unfruitful. The future looks good. And there's a plant but no fruit. This person is not a hard person, like the wayside soil. Nor is he shallow like the rocky soil. The thorny ground person is the undecided person who wants both worlds. He wants Jesus and the world too. The ladder of his life is on the wall of wealth and things.

Jesus describes him in verse 22: "The one who received the seed that fell among the thorns is the man who hears the Word, but the worries of this life and the deceitfulness of wealth choke it, making it unfruitful."

As we witness faithfully, the scattered seed will often fall into these kinds of soil—wayside, rocky, and thorn-infested soil. We need to understand and be prepared for unresponsive people. However, the good news is that there are also three kinds of *good soil.*

THE GOOD SOIL

"Still other seed fell on good soil, where it produced a crop—a hundred, sixty or thirty times what was sown" (v. 8). Just as there are three kinds of bad soil, so there are three types of good soil.

Some soil is so exceptional that it yields a hundredfold. Still other soil will produce sixtyfold, while some soil brings forth thirtyfold. Remember that the yield of the harvest is dependent on the quality of the soil.

It is important to realize that all believers bear some fruit from time to time. If there is no fruit, then we would do well to examine ourselves regarding the reality of our conversion. We all bear fruit . . . some thirtyfold, some sixtyfold, and some a hundredfold. Our number one concern is not how much fruit we bear, but that we *faithfully* sow the good seed.

But someone responds, "By nature I'm very shy. I'm an introvert." Or, "I'm a new Christian; I've had no experience." The challenge from Jesus is sow the good seed anyway. "Yes, but I'm just an average Jane or Joe." The point is not your ability, intelligence, or charisma, it is the divine power of the seed and the Spirit-prepared soil that brings fruit. Results are God's prerogative, while faithfulness is ours.

It's that simple. Each of us is to witness *faithfully*. That's it — that's our assignment as given by Jesus. We are commanded to witness faithfully by sowing the seed of the Gospel.

REMINDERS
● "The Sower" is *anyone* who shares the Gospel and "the seed" is the *message* of salvation.
● No human being scatters seed perfectly. Some seed will fall upon poor soil, regardless of our skill or lack of skill.
● The rocky soil person is one who responds with an enthusiasm that looks like the real thing, but there's no root.
● The thorny ground person is the undecided person who wants both worlds.
● All Christians bear some fruit from time to time.
● Results are God's prerogative while ours is faithfulness.

Oftentimes, excusing of a fault
Doth make the fault the worse by excuse;
As patches set upon a little breach,
Discredit more in the hiding of the fault,
Than did the fault before it was so patched.

> William Shakespeare (*King John*, Act IV,
> Scene 2)

And they all with one consent began to make excuses.

> Luke 14:18

I saw that it was better to make a mistake in one's first effort
at personal spiritual conversation, and correct that mistake
afterwards, than not to make any effort. There can be no mistake so bad, in working for an individual soul for Christ, as
the fatal mistake of not making an honest endeavor. How
many persons refrain from doing anything lest they possibly
should do the wrong thing just now! Not doing is the worst
of doing.

> Henry Clay Trumbull (in book by his son,
> C.G. Trumbull, *Taking Men Alive,* Fleming
> H. Revell, p. 55)

THIRTEEN
Please Excuse Me

F or many of us, making excuses is a way of life. It's just about as common as taking a breath of air or going to sleep at night. In the cartoon strip "Peanuts," Lucy blames missing a flying baseball on the sun, the moon, the wind, the stars, and even the toxic substance in her baseball glove.

WHAT IS AN EXCUSE?
We make excuses for all kinds of things. Some of the most common heard by ministers are the excuses for not attending church. The weather keeps some away. Either it is too hot, too cold, too wet, or it's just too nice. Whatever the explanation, often it's a cover-up for neglect. In other words, it's an excuse.

What is an excuse? *The Random House Dictionary* defines it as any attempt "to regard or judge with indulgence . . . to pardon or forgive" one's actions.

It is my opinion that there is a difference between a reason and an excuse. A reason is something we give before a conclusion is reached. It is an underlying fact that provides logic for a decision. An excuse is something we give for not completing the action. Reasons are usually sincere. Excuses generally are rationalizations. A reason is for the most part real, whereas an excuse is an invention, or at best, a very weak reason.

WHY DO WE MAKE EXCUSES?

There are probably as many "reasons" as there are people for excuse making. But as we examine this question, we discover several possibilities.

The excuse of lack of ability. Many people make excuses because they lack confidence. These people are often timid. The Bible gives an illustration of this in Exodus 3. There we have the picture of Moses telling God why he can't serve. "Who am I, that I should go to Pharaoh and bring the Israelites out of Egypt?" (v. 11)

Later Moses excused himself again, saying, " 'O Lord, I have never been eloquent, neither in the past nor since You have spoken to Your servant. I am slow of speech and tongue.' The Lord said to him, 'Who gave man his mouth? Who makes him deaf or mute? Who gave him sight or makes him blind? Is it not I, the Lord? Now go; I will help you speak and will teach you what to say' " (Ex. 4:10-12).

Moses felt inferior. "The roof of my mouth gets dry," he appears to say. "My tongue won't move, my knees knock, I am not eloquent, and I can't be Your witness."

I can understand that. I've felt the same way many times. Often I have questioned my gifts, but the Lord seemed to say, "Go on, keep going on, and I will be with you." Lay hold of the promise of God's abiding presence and witness faithfully.

For the most part, it is not those who have the greatest gifts who get the most done. D.L. Moody had only a fifth-grade education, but he became God's instrument to move people of two continents in the direction of heaven. When God wants to get a job done, He doesn't seem to look for a person with extraordinary talents or abilities. Rather, He looks for a person who is committed. When God created man, He began with dirt, not diamonds. When He gave instructions for building the tabernacle, He specified that it was to be built with boards and badger skins. God appears to delight in using ordinary things. He looks for someone who is willing to do anything, go anywhere, and pay any price to do His will. I find encouragement in the phrase, "Little is much, when God is in it."

The best way to get started is simply to get started. Don't mull over all the pros and cons of the job. Don't analyze an alibi—just begin. The Lord will use your efforts no matter how weak you might think them to be.

The excuse of blaming others. The graffiti on the old brick tenement building offered a variety of messages to those passing. Among them, in bold, black letters: "Humpty Dumpty was pushed."

Shifting responsibility is a common excuse. Human beings for centuries have been shifting responsibility to others. In Genesis 3 we read about the failure of Adam and Eve. "But the Lord God called to the man, 'Where are you?' He answered, 'I heard You in the garden, and I was afraid because I was naked; so I hid.' And He said, 'Who told you that you were naked? Have you eaten from the tree that I commanded you not to eat from?' The man said, 'The woman You put here with me—she gave me some fruit from the tree, and I ate it.' Then the Lord God said to the woman, 'What is this you have done?' The woman said, 'The serpent deceived me, and I ate' " (3:9-13).

Adam's first response was to blame Eve and God, all in one breath. "The woman You put here with me—she gave me some fruit." Adam used Eve as an excuse, but he also blamed God. It's as if he were saying, "After all, Lord, You gave me this woman; it's really Your fault!"

Of course, Eve wasn't any better. She did the very same thing. She said, "The serpent deceived me" (v. 13). She also shifted the blame.

The real reason for Adam's and Eve's sin had nothing to do with those excuses. Verse 6 of the same chapter points out that when Eve looked upon the tree, she saw that it was good for food. She saw that it was pleasant to the eyes. She desired it to make her wise. She yielded to the temptation and took the fruit. Adam and Eve hid behind excuses, and that's all they were— excuses! The root of their disobedience was selfishness.

A businessman told me that he could not witness because of an unsympathetic wife. I encouraged him to be sensitive to his wife, but suggested that possibly he was hiding behind his wife as an excuse. With a little thought and creativity, he could witness in many situations that would not involve his wife.

A woman told me that as a homemaker her opportunities were so limited that witnessing was not possible. I suggested that she invite her neighbors in for a coffee time or a cookie exchange, a Bible study, or that she just enclose appropriate, attractive literature as she paid her bills. If we sincerely want to witness, we will find opportunities. Too often we evade our calling by blaming others.

One of the most common examples of blame shifting is the person who says he is not a Christian or a witnessing Christian because there are so many hypocrites in the church. This too is an excuse! That's like a dying man saying, "I would go to the hospital for help if there just weren't so many sick people there." Sad to say, there are hypocrites in every church just as there are hypocrites in every area of life. But it's dishonest to minimize the faithful who are honestly serving and magnify those who are hypocritical.

Paul writes, "So then, each of us will give an account of himself to God" (Rom. 14:12). We will not have to answer for others. We will have to answer for ourselves! Shifting the blame is not only false; it can be fatal.

The excuse of being too busy. "I'm doing too much already" is the excuse of some. But there's a difference between busyness and truly being busy. Some look and sound busy but in reality they are unorganized. They waste time and fail to get things done, while others are lazy and often excuse their laziness by calling those with more energy fanatics.

There's another group of people, however, who really are too busy. Jesus talked about them in His Parable of the Great Supper (Luke 14). Speaking to the religious leaders of His day, Jesus told the story of a man who planned a dinner party and invited many guests.

"Jesus replied: 'A certain man was preparing a great banquet and invited many guests. At the time of the banquet he sent his servant to tell those who had been invited, 'Come, for everything is now ready.' But they all alike began to make excuses. The first said, 'I have just bought a field, and I must go and see it. Please excuse me.' Another said, 'I have just bought five yoke of oxen, and I'm on my way to try them out. Please excuse me.' Still another said, 'I just got married, so I can't come' " (Luke 14:16-20).

Consider several interesting observations. First, this supper was a special occasion, and the guests had *previously* been invited. Verse 17 says that they "had been invited." The guests had been honored probably well in advance with an invitation to attend.

Second, we can rightly determine that these people who had been "invited" to the feast were now just being summoned. In other words, these in all likelihood had already consented to come. They were simply waiting for the announcement that the feast was ready to start.

Third, unfortunately we find that all three of the men excused themselves and refused to attend the dinner.

The first one said, "I have just bought a field and I must go and see it" (v. 18). What a weak excuse. If he had been a good businessman, he would have visited the land before he bought it. Furthermore, he had already purchased the land; it was not going anywhere. He could just as well have visited his property after the dinner. He apparently was too involved with his possessions. But in reality, his answer is nothing more than an excuse.

The second man also excused himself because he was too busy. He had purchased five yoke of oxen, and he wanted to go prove them. This man's excuse was inadequate for the same reasons. Why had he not proven his animals before the dinner, or for that matter, why could they not wait until later? His excuse was, of course, just an alibi.

But what about the third man? His excuse was the most ridiculous of all. He had just been married. This man, like the others, had promised ahead of time that he would attend. Could he not have brought his wife with him? The new bride probably would have enjoyed the party!

Each of these delinquent guests illustrates the fact that our feet follow our heart. Regardless of circumstances, we generally do what we want to do.

WHAT DOES THE BIBLE SAY ABOUT EXCUSES?

Adam and Eve were judged and expelled from the Garden. The master of the feast, in Luke 14, was angry, and all those who made excuses were excluded — "Not one of those men who were invited will get a taste of my banquet" (v. 24).

Occasionally, I have said, "Excuses only satisfy the people who make them." And for the most part, that's true. When we excuse ourselves we really *accuse ourselves*. Alexander Pope characterized excuses severely. "An excuse," he wrote, "is more terrible than a lie, for an excuse is a lie guarded." Excuses can be lies that masquerade as legitimate reasons and therefore are doubly wrong.

But, of course, the most important concern is what does God think of excuses. Do they satisfy Him? God calls us to serve Him faithfully. Just as the master of the feast was angry when his guests spurned him, so God is grieved when we fail to obey Him, and excuse ourselves.

It is encouraging to remember that the God who *calls us* to witness promises to give us the ability to do it (Phil. 4:13). He never asks us to do what we cannot do. Witnessing is *do-able.* "And God is able to make all grace abound to you" (2 Cor. 9:8).

REMINDERS
- Reasons are usually sincere. Excuses are generally insincere rationalizations.
- God delights to use the simple things of life. When God made man, He used dirt, not diamonds. When He gave instructions for building the tabernacle, He specified that it was to be built with boards and badger skins.
- The best way to get started in witnessing is simply to get started.
- When we excuse ourselves, we really accuse ourselves.
- Excuses satisfy only the people who make them.
- "An excuse is more terrible than a lie, for an excuse is a lie guarded" (Alexander Pope).

As long as it is day, we must do the work of Him who sent Me. Night is coming, when no one can work.

John 9:4

Samuel Zwemer once addressed a student convention on the needs of the Islamic world, and closed his appeal by walking over to a great map of the Muslim lands. Spreading his arms over it, he said, "Thou, O Christ, art all I need, and Thou, O Christ, are all they need." He is our urgency.

Leighton Ford (*The Christian Persuader*, Harper & Row, p. 40)

I believe that if an angel were to wing his way from earth up to Heaven, and were to say that there was one poor, ragged boy, without father or mother, with no one to care for him and teach him the way of life; and if God were to ask who among them were willing to come down to this earth and live here for fifty years and lead that one to Jesus Christ, every angel in Heaven would volunteer to go. Even Gabriel, who stands in the presence of the Almighty, would say, "Let me leave my high and lofty position, and let me have the luxury of leading one soul to Jesus Christ." There is no greater honor than to be the instrument in God's hands of leading one person out of the kingdom of Satan into the glorious light of Heaven.

D.L. Moody

FOURTEEN

God's Urgency

Have you ever thought of God as being in a hurry? Probably not. Too often we think of God as having little or no concern with passing time. And yet the message of urgency runs through the entire Bible. A good question might be, Is God ever in a hurry?

During Jesus' earthly ministry, He gave an illustration that conveys something of God's concern for those who have gone astray. While speaking to a crowd of religious leaders, Jesus told the story of a prodigal son (Luke 15). That young man rebelled against his father just as we have rebelled against God the Heavenly Father. The prodigal son insisted on his own way of "riotous living." Ultimately, the parable tells how he squandered his inheritance, recognized his sin, and decided to return to his father and home.

The father appears to be a picture of God the Father waiting and watching for His Son's return. The Scriptures say, "But while he was still a long way off, his father saw him and was filled with compassion for him; he *ran* to his son, threw his arms around him and kissed him" (Luke 15:20).

The eyes of love were swifter than the feet of repentance. The father saw his son, had compassion, *and ran* to welcome him home again. The compassionate father was in a hurry to receive his wayward son.

J.B. Phillips translates verses 22-24 as " 'Hurry!' called out his father to the servants, 'fetch the best clothes and put them on him! Put a ring on his finger and shoes on his feet, and get that fatted calf and kill it, and we will have a feast and a celebration! For this is my son—he was dead, and he's alive again.' " The father not only hurried to welcome his son home but required haste in preparing a party to celebrate.

On another occasion Jesus said, "As long as it is day, we must do the work of Him who sent Me. Night is coming, when no one can work" (John 9:4). Even though Jesus was God, He was conscious of the limitations of time. We humans have only a few years to witness, and then the night comes. Our witnessing days are not forever.

THE RESURRECTION

Although Jesus repeatedly told His disciples of His coming resurrection, they were unprepared. On the resurrection morning, God's angel appeared and spoke to the women at the tomb. "He is not here; He has risen, just as He said. Come and see the place where He lay. Then go quickly and tell His disciples: 'He has risen from the dead' " (Matt. 28:6-7).

"Go quickly." How were the women to go? The message of the resurrection called for haste. Mary Magdalene and the other women (see Luke 24:10) told Peter and John, and they ran together to the sepulcher (John 20:4).

THE EARLY CHURCH

When the angel of the Lord directed Philip to witness to the Ethiopian eunuch, "Philip ran" (Acts 8:30).

Paul teaches that all Christians must make "the most of every opportunity, because the days are evil" (Eph. 5:16). He encouraged young Timothy to "fan into flame the gift of God, which is in you" (2 Tim. 1:6). Paul was saying, "Fight the fading flame; don't get cold." I have noticed that it takes effort to get a hot fire going.

In the last book of the Bible, we note the call to readiness and witness. "I am coming soon. Hold on to what you have, so that no one will take your crown" (Rev. 3:11).

J.I. Packer pointedly comments, "Whatever we may believe about election, the fact remains that men without Christ are lost, and going to hell.... 'Except ye repent,' said our Lord to the crowd, 'ye shall all ... perish.' And we who are Christ's are sent to tell them of the One—the only One—who can save them from perishing. Is not their need urgent? ... Does that not make evangelism a matter of urgency for us?" (*Evangelism and the Sovereignty of God*, InterVarsity Press, p. 98).

The words of instruction and warning in Revelation 3:11 are followed with the illustration of a lukewarm church that had lost its urgency.

An alarm is sounded. "I know your deeds, that you are neither cold nor hot. I wish you were either one or the other! So, because you are lukewarm—neither hot nor cold—I am about to spit you out of My mouth" (3:15-16).

"You are lukewarm—neither cold nor hot." A sleeping Christian is no contest for a white-hot world. A comfortable, cozy Christian in Sleepy Valley in all probability will not witness faithfully.

Jesus is saying, "Wake up! Work while it is day."

Probably the greatest problem facing the church today is the number of lukewarm, uninvolved Christians who neglect to witness concerning Jesus Christ. At times it seems as though some have a mild case of Christianity, as though they've been vaccinated against the real thing. In a world on fire, lukewarmness is an affront to God.

What happened 1,200 years ago to the church in Africa? It failed to be a mission force and became a mission field. What happened to the church in Russia a half century ago? Saltless and lightless, it became ineffective. Having no sense of urgency, they drifted to death.

I have heard a fictitious story about a farmer who was awakened in the middle of the night when his alarm clock struck seventeen. Confused, he hurried through the house calling, "Wake up! Wake up! It's later than it's ever been before!"

In reality, it is later than it ever has been before.

An assessment is made. The problem with the church of Laodicea is found in two phrases, "You say . . . and do not realize" (v. 17). Those are not pretty words, and there's no way to make them attractive. "You say, 'I am rich; I have acquired wealth and do not need a thing.' But you do not realize that you are wretched, pitiful, poor, blind and naked." That is not the assessment of any individual, but of the all-knowing God.

Action is required. "Those whom I love I rebuke and discipline. So be earnest, and repent. Here I am! I stand at the door and knock. If anyone hears My voice and opens the door, I will come in and eat with him, and he with Me" (3:19-20).

"Be earnest." The word *earnest* means "devoted, fervent, passionate, warm, and spirit-directed."

"You lack a sense of urgency," Jesus is saying. "You show little compassion. It is time to repent!"

Commenting on the word *repent*, the famous preacher Alexander MacLaren told his congregation that in repentance "there must be a lowly consciousness of sin, a clear vision of past shortcomings . . . an abhorrence of these, and joined with that, a resolute act of mind and heart beginning a new course, and a change of purpose."

In other words, repentance means more than just feeling bad about the past; real repentance *leads to a new commitment.*

Archbishop William Temple once said, "When people complain that the church should *do something,* they usually mean that the pastor should *say something."* Our sin has been that we talk too much and do too little.

It is time that we who are the church of Jesus Christ begin to feel and understand God's urgency. That little couplet is true, "Only one life, 'twill soon be past. Only what's done for Christ will last."

The time to witness is now—not tomorrow or next month, or next year—it is now!

Every old-time circus had a barker who promoted each attraction. He would call out, "Hurry! Hurry! Hurry!" And people would rush to some trivial sideshow.

At times in my subconscious I seem to hear the voice of God calling, "Hurry! Hurry! Hurry, for those I love die so fast." The call is not to some passing earthly side show, but to the main issue of time and eternity. Even now the Spirit of God is calling, "Stir up your gift. Redeem the time. Work while it is day. Hurry! Hurry! Hurry!"

REMINDERS
● I have noticed that a hot fire burns easily, but a weak one struggles all the way.
● A comfortable, cozy Christian in Sleepy Valley will never evangelize.
● At times it seems as though some believers have a mild case of Christianity, and respond as though they've been vaccinated against the real thing.
● "When people complain that the church should do something, they usually mean that the pastor should say something" (Archbishop William Temple).
● "Only one life, 'twill soon be past. Only what's done for Christ will last."
● At times, I sense the inner voice of God calling, "Hurry! Hurry! Hurry, for those I love die so fast."

	DATE DUE		
3/14/96			

```
Sweeting, George          248.
The no-guilt guide        5
    to witnessing         SWE
```